Redefining Masculinity

Davidson Nguyen Hang

with Edwin C. Aristor, Joseph A. Bologna,
Ryan D. Hall, Mark Hunter, Peter McLean,
Christopher Paige, Alex Terranova,
and Kevin Wilhelm

Green Heart Living Press

Redefining Masculinity

ISBN (paperback): 978-1-954493-04-9

ISBN (ebook): 978-1-954493-05-6

Edited by Elizabeth B. HIll, MSW & Jaime L. Williams

Cover photo credit: Joseph Bologna

Dedication

I want to dedicate this to my father. Without him I would simply not be alive. I would have probably not been involved with Streetwise Partners, Orphans Futures Alliance, BuildOn, IMentor, Exploring Paths, and Pencil. Your lack of presence in my life over the last 18 years has been transformative. My healing process began four years ago with Accomplishment Coaching. Since then, I would never have imagined the beautiful life I have now, because I tried so hard to make up for lost time. I had to prove to the world that I am worthy of your love. I know now that self-acceptance is key.

Table of Contents

Acknowledgments

I am grateful for every single human being who has made a difference in my life.

Garrett Rafols - whose listening is all it takes to feel connected to the world.

Mark Hunter - thank you for your contributions and for standing for each and every one of us at Accomplishment Coaching. Antonio Brasse, Alex Terranova, Neil Goldstein, Ryan Long, Randy Gornitzky, Aaron Boykin, Jeff Zacharski, Frank Bonomo, and Jason Dukes, you have all been the clearing example of men that have helped me not to be afraid to show my emotions. I cried 180 days out of the 365 days during the program, and I wouldn't have it any other way.

Laura Westman, Alex Terranova, Jason Dukes, and Mark Hunter - your coaching has been instrumental in my healing to be fully present in my marriage and with my family.

The brothers of Pi Delta Psi especially Tommy Tran, Phuong Huynh, Than Nguyen, and my best friend Davis Huang. You have all taught me the meaning of brotherhood.

My mother, grandmother, uncles, and sisters - I'm sorry it took me so long to be able to see the beauty in each and every one of you.

The Landmark family- Trevor Price and Kevin Ko - my coaches from Landmark who held the space while I made every excuse in the book to run away from family - it's the thing that calls me the most.

Being able to see other men cry and be able to process their deepest darkest emotions. Shout out to the Fellas Aditya Guthey, Brandon Ngai, Edwin Aristor, Nick Pan, Jeff Zacharski, Juan De Angulo, Nick Singh, Spencer White, William Lee, Mike Liguori, and Juan David. The men's group that I created has given me so much. I cannot describe in words what you mean to me. Seeing everyone open up and share their hearts so openly gives me optimism that there is a new wave of men who are not afraid to love and not afraid to show their weaknesses.

My beautiful wife - Samantha Chang is so patient with me. She helps me see what's possible by working on and being committed to our family. She touches me and shows me what unconditional love looks like. I may not be perfect, but I feel pretty close to being perfect when I'm with you.

My mother - I love you so much. Thank you for coming to America where all of your kids are thriving, and we can have freedom and choices.

To the other contributing authors Mark Hunter, Alex Terranova, Ryan Hall, Kevin Wilhelm, Joseph Bologna, Edwin Aristor, Christopher Paige, and Peter McLean, thank you.

Thank you to Chris Wong and Thomas Wang for being my first two coaches. Although my time with you both was short, you introduced me into this beautiful world called personal responsibility.

All of this would not be possible without the incredible and loving Elizabeth Hill. You have shown us what's possible through collaboration, love, joy, and trusting your intuition. Special shout out to the Green Heart Living team, Jaime Williams and Casey Banville, for their contributions and edits. I never thought I would be a writer, but with your support, anything is possible.

Introduction

Davidson Nguyen Hang

The reason why I wanted to put this project together was because I was a product of masculinity gone wrong. Unfortunately, my father never had a place to process his feelings and emotions. I've spent the last 18 years of my life without a father and wanted to be the opposite of him. That's not an empowering way to live life. Over the past four years, I have learned to accept him and that he did the best he could given the circumstances.

To provide context, my father moved to America at a young age and worked through racism. He was a street vendor. You know those people you come across when walking through any city? They sell watches, gloves, scarves. He was robbed and had many things stolen from him. One memorable story was that he had a truck full of merchandise stolen from him. He had over $15k worth of merchandise stolen that had taken us many months to get.

I have seen how many men are not able to process their emotions because of societal norms and cultural values. I started taking a different path after attending some men's groups. I was always an emotional person. I'm not sure why that is, but I was told that I would cling to my dad when I was a baby and cry anytime he put me down.

It shattered my heart when he left us without saying a word. He moved to California when I was a sophomore in high school. Since then, I've had many good role models such as Michael Liguori Senior, Bill Jones, Tommy Tran, and many brothers in my Asian Cultural Fraternity, Pi Delta Psi. These role models have had a significant influence on me growing up.

Creating a safe space where men can cry, lean on each other, and open up about personal issues that come up is freeing and can be life-changing. In the men's group that I have created, it has been heartwarming to see all of us open up about our insecurities and celebrate each other's victories and accomplishments.

Thank you for taking the time to be curious. Thank you for your commitment to growing and serving the families around you. With this book, I challenge you to start opening up more about your insecurities and to have deep conversations with the people around you. You'll be surprised at how we all crave these intimate conversations, and you could be the one who initiates all of this magical beauty.

Dear Reader

Peter McLean

Lets look at a poem together.

Maybe there's something hidden in here that you, dear reader, will see and share and bring to sweet life.

We are all approaching the fire,
each on our own path toward this circle of wild hearts.

The birds lift from the forest floor as your feet fall on
the oak leaves soon to be soil.

Your deft steps on proud rocks that crest the river's surface
keeping your boots dry and spirits high.

Your toes, dirt dark and deft. Heels, hard pads generous and
tough.

Your feet are telling you of what you value.

The calluses that once were blisters are now the love
children, the wedding consecration, of Longing and Leaving,
and their gifts: turning rocks and thorns as smooth and soft
as moss.

You've left.
Certainly.

You'll return.
Hopefully.

But not as you were.

As something you can't quite know just yet.
And more on that later.

But these stars need to drift and slide a little first.
And the new coals, hidden in those oak logs split and stacked,
by men days ago, for you, for your leaving, for your returning,
are not yet aglow in this once in a life fire.

But again, more on what you've left, who you're becoming,
and where you'll return to:
Later.

For now: the ache in your shoulders and lower back, all good signposts on your journey to here, to now,
to this fire that's been burning for you.

Now, look around the circle.

Look at the faces. The eyes.

These are your brothers. Your cherished companions.

Take them in.

Stand.

Admire them.

Their eyes. Noses. Ears. Hair. Chests. Arms. Legs. Feet. Faces.

Receive them.

Drink from them. Their strength. Courage. Bravery. Might. Tenderness. Sensitivity. Trustworthiness. Their

Wounds. Their Wisdom. Their Grief.

Feel the oneness.

Now.
Turn around to face the darkness.
And take the darkness in.
Take in the darkness with your eyes. Shadows. Forms. Fire light playing on leaves of trees there and not.

Now your ears.
Send your ears out to the top of the near ridge.
To the river running in its banks. To the owls silent strike. To the doe nibbling and her two spotted fauns too playful for this hour.

Now your nose.
Breathe in the darkness. Breathe her in. Her wisdom. Her depth.
That's the smell of soul out there.
That's the smell of crooked and bent, wild and winding.
Get familiar.

Now use your skin and hair to feel her.
Her movements. Her breath. Her temperature.
Humidity. Your toes on the earth. Feeling her vibrations.

The Darkness is your teacher.
Faithful. Constant. Consistent. Not to be afraid of, but to be cautious in, for sure.

Close your eyes. Feel the fire on your calves. Your hamstrings. Butt. Lower back. Upper back. Hands. Arms. Neck. And in your hair.

Now feel the darkness on your brow. Your nose. The cool of the in-breath. Her touch on your cheek, shoulders, chest, stomach, arms, hands, legs, knees, shins, toes.

Walk forward one step and stand.
Stand and feel.

Feel the THIS.

The THISNESS.

The unique, never before ever in your entire life feeling on your body right now.

The play of heat and night.

Use every receptor you have available to you to feel the continental cosmic and quantum shift that that single step made in your life.

Feel it. Breathe it.
One more step forward.
Feel the darkness at your front. The distant fire at your back.

Do I feel the fire? Or is that the memory of its feel?
Do I feel the darkness? Or am I convincing myself?
Return to your ears. Send them far, high, low and near.

To your nose. The cool air in your nostrils. The smell of cool moist air. Of firs and furs. Caves and coves.

What do you smell when you let yourself fully inhabit your nose?

One more step.
One more time.
One more acquainting.
One more meeting.
One more awakening to this new land you find yourself in.

Feel the acuity of your senses.
Welcome them.
They've been waiting for you.
You've been waiting for them.
You'll need them. Where you're going.
Your life depends on it.

You are not alone but you'll need to walk your path alone.
At least for now.

The acorn doesn't take suggestions, defer to the committee,
or ask a fortune teller when beginning to grow.

The white tail buck does not consult the focus group on the
riverine growth of his rack. He just eats, sleeps, fucks, and
pushes that shit out with wild and reckless artisanship.

But the oak and buck must grow and age in the company of
other acorn droppers and other antler adorned.

And they cannot become their fullest expression without
knowing their own true path,
their own unique song,
their own smell,
their own dance, flow, rhythm, rock, sway, skip, pop, hop,
hoot, howl, growl, bowel, jump into the river of your own life
and refuse the towel, grab a fat kid by the face and kiss him
on his jowl, yell out in orgasmic grunts consisting of only the
ancient vowels.

You are a unique and beautiful mystery unto yourself.

And there is more to you than you know.
More parts.

Just as your senses found the depth of the forest when

finally, they were asked and enlivened.

In the same way, the depth of you has yet to be fully seen, smelled, felt, tasted, and acknowledged.

And now begins your courtship.

The bouquets tied with silk, intended to bring these unknown, disowned, emaciated-skin-and-bone parts of yourself back home.
Back castle.
Back forest.
Back river.
Back shore.
Back heart.
Back soul.
Back brothers!
Back!
Back into beautiful union with the whole night sky a-lit in each one of you.

You gotta leave though.
You gotta go.
And it's this choiceless choice of severance that will begin your trip back home to yourself,
the new self, the integrated self, the self containing constellations not yet seen but anciently known.

Kabier says, "The longing does the work."
So, reach down and touch your feet.
Trace the pads of your toes and heels.
Feel that.
That is the result of the longing.
Did you set out for calluses? Was that the scent you caught on the wind? Calluses?
Or was it a wild life of love and passion, creation, protection, service, exhilaration,

*to live rightly and playfully and in deep respect with all things
living and to extend the construct of living well beyond what
our society has taught us about animate or inanimate?
What are you longing for?*

What are you longing for?

*Who is depending on you following and trusting that longing?
What is at stake if you don't step slowly away from that fire?
If you don't step out, slowly, to meet your teacher,
the Darkness?*

*Look around.
See what you've attracted into your life.
See what you are making happen. With these men. These
humans. These beings.
With this fire. With these stars. These trees. These brothers.*

*Your mothers, sisters, brothers, fathers, lovers, grandfathers
and grandmothers are calling and singing and cheering you
as you make the long journey back home to yourself.*

The above is a poem written to inspire those that know they
have to leave. What are they leaving? The standard
expression of humanity today. The standard expression of
masculinity today. The standard expression of being an
office worker today. The standard expression of how to have
sex today. The standard expression of how to listen today.
The standard expression of what it means to be a human in
all of our vast beauty and diversity while recognizing our
place in a world made up of way way way way way more
than humans. Recognizing the tiny sliver of the pie that we
make up as humans in this great earthly web.

The standard expression of today is so life draining and the
poet knows it, sees it, speaks to it, and is working their poet's
damnedest to encourage those who must leave the shore of

their standard expressions and enter the dark waters of not knowing. Knowing, and the need to know, is one of the greatest hurdles to finding out what stands between you and your fullest expression. Because. There is no way to know. Knowing won't arrive. And when it does. It's no longer relevant. But goddamn do we cling to knowing. Goddamn do we want certainty. Goddamn do we organize ruthlessly around safety, security, and predictability.

All things in moderation.

The recipe calls for a dash of Safety. Not three and half cups.

And as men, as beautiful male-bodied babes, we have this internal pull in us (and not that our female bodied sisters and aunties don't) to move between the poles of safety and security and quest and adventure. Neither end of the continuum is better than the other. AND, our modern American culture has prioritized the safety and security pole and has demonized the quest and adventure pole. Neither one is better than the other. The question most concerning me is the What For, the Why? What For all that safety and security? Who for? What For all that questing and adventuring? Who for? Are these positions along the poles serving you? Serving just your family? Serving your community? Serving healing and reconnection and mending of societal and cultural relationships?

That's what I want to hear the poet speak to, riff on, chatter on about. What for? Why go into the darkness? Who for? What changes in the world when our men leave the warmth of the fire and quest into the darkness? And let's say these men have a quest in mind, in heart, that looks to serve the whole. What would the world start looking like, sounding like, feeling like, grieving like, if the Who For, What For, Why was dialed in a little more to something beyond me and mine and accumulation and status and power?

Come on, dear poet, if I put another log on, then will you sing?

If I put another log on, fill up your mug, and hand you the blanket my mother quilted, then will you? For I want to know. I'm dying to know.

Mark Hunter, MCC, 53

Charlotte, Vermont

Chapter 1

The Masculinity Myth

Mark Hunter, MCC

Masculinity has been called everything from "the source of modern civilization" and a revered quality that equates with success and strength, to "toxic" and dangerous, a form of emotional weakness, the main reason for all the ills in the world, and a thing to be shunned.

The truth is that it has been, and is, all of those things at once.

Masculinity is both an aspect of our humanity and a contextual orientation to our external world that often "feels good" in its most toxic forms as much as (or more than) its effective forms. It most often manipulates a version of strength that's fundamentally hierarchical and oppositional in nature.

Masculinity is an aspect of every human being - male or female - and it's designed to emote a presence of power, unstoppable-ness, and invulnerability. The cost is that it's often accompanied by an absence of empathy, humanity, and care. In this way, masculinity, in its "toxic" cultural form, is both one of the biggest existential problems we face as a species and, at the same time, the solution to that very same existential problem.

Conscious Ferocity

Toxic masculinity most typically refers to the aggressive,

violent, unemotional alpha male that also stereotypically devalues women, is centered around competition, power (both physical and social), unhealthy risk-taking, and celebrated promiscuity. It's also widely addressed as one of the main issues behind violence (on both local and global levels), and anxiety amongst adolescent males.[1] None of this is inaccurate.

The issue is that it's taught to boys overtly (the suppression of emotion, striving for and maintenance of dominance, promiscuity, self-reliance and showing strength above all else), and it's learned by women who want to succeed in environments where that same "toxic" masculinity is celebrated and rewarded. I was readily taught these things as a young boy myself – as much by osmosis through the media and my environment than by anything direct.

I do, however, specifically recall being shamed for crying, for losing, for needing help, for appearing to care too much about anything or anyone, for studying hard at school, and for appearing weak in any form, for any reason. I remember that the boys who did not learn this lesson were ostracized and regarded publicly as something "less than a man." I also recall seeing movies, books and television that celebrated masculinity at its worst, and watched men (and some women) all around me succeed by adopting those traits, so much so that I recall thinking that it had more to do with power, toughness and winning than it had to do just with me being male. It was inescapable, and it permeated all aspects of the world I lived in and still live in.[2]

Most recently, the "#MeToo" movement has elevated the masculinity conversation (more accurately the "toxic masculinity" conversation) by highlighting what's most

---

[1] Dr. Tali Shenfield, "A Primer on Child And Adolescent Anxiety," Advanced Psychology, April 2015.
[2] Kirsten Weir, "The Men America Left Behind," American Psychological Association, February 2017.

damaging about it in its most extreme form. None of that is inaccurate, it's just not the complete picture that the solution requires us to consider; "masculinity" is a part of every single one of us, and we need to focus on what to do *with* it from here because it isn't going away.

Additionally, "masculinity" gets too easily collapsed with "toxic masculinity" whenever convenient to the narrative, especially in the media. Masculinity needs to be worked WITH instead of trying to eradicate it, relating to it as inherently "toxic," blaming it for everything wrong in the world or simply replacing it with the feminine. These "solutions" are overly simplistic and reactionary…interestingly, both these issues with these "solutions" represent examples of a toxic-masculine reaction to toxic masculinity itself.

The problem with simply blanket-vilifying masculinity and trying to eradicate or replace it with the feminine, in addition to it simply being lazy and reactionary to do so, is two-fold: first, it's not inherently "bad," it's simply misused. Second, it's falsely depicted as a trait associated only with men, and is almost always only addressed as such. In truth, it's a trait directly associated with power and success (accurately or not) and one that has been adopted by men and women alike in order to achieve success in the corporate world and other environments where the traditional persona of power and strength are still revered and directly rewarded.

Simply vilifying masculinity as inherently "toxic" misses these nuances and leaves us all without the awareness needed to address the real issue: *Fear*. Specifically, the fear of the ego being revealed and disarmed, and thereby wounded. If we take a close look, the "toxic" aspects of masculinity almost always arise in the presence of a perceived threat to its dominance or control. That's exactly what I was taught as a kid: *"be afraid of being seen as weak."* Whether you are a man or a woman reading this, the part of you that attacks when your ego is threatened, or becomes "toxic" to those around you when you feel your imagined sense of control slipping away in a situation, is your own "toxic masculinity" at work.

The problem arises in that you use this fear-response not just when your life is at risk (like at 3 am in a dark alley, which is what it was designed for on an evolutionary basis), but you also use it when you feel like your perceived status, power or sense of self is threatened, and that can happen in many places where the automatic fear reaction isn't necessarily appropriate (like at 2pm on a Tuesday in your team meeting at work when someone disagrees with you.)

Simply vilifying masculinity for this is the contextual equivalent of vilifying hammers because they often get used to break things. That's factually true, but they're a tool that's designed to build as well as to break, and they can be wielded by anyone, with either purpose. So, hammers aren't good or bad, right or wrong, they're a tool. The REAL issue is who's using the hammer and what are they using it for? In answering this most important question, character matters most.

Character Matters Most

The one who wields their masculinity is the source of the choice to use it in service of creation, relationship and stand, or for violence, separation and force. This choice is most readily predicted by the character of the individual using it.

In the foreword to his book *The Road To Character*, David Brooks says that, "Although we are flawed creatures, we are also splendidly endowed...We are both weak and strong, bound and free, blind and far seeing. We thus have the capacity to struggle with ourselves...In the struggle against your own weakness, humility is the greatest virtue."[3]

---

[3] David Brooks, *The Road to Character.*

It is this struggle with masculine in each of us that is the epicenter of the next evolution of our species. It is the humility of this struggle that creates the space for the masculine to become a tool of creation rather than destruction. Brooks goes on to beautifully describe character as being "built in the course of your inner confrontation." This "inner confrontation" he speaks to is not between the masculine and the feminine aspects in each of us, but between the ego and the fear of it being revealed and damaged, that masculinity is too often the solution to.

If we took this approach to masculinity, there would be no more need to address "toxic masculinity" and instead we'd be talking about the toxic expression of fear. THAT conversation could change the world, but reducing it to a problem of masculinity misses the big picture; that we have succumbed to our avoidance of fear itself, and will do anything to escape the experience of it. "Toxic Masculinity" is just one large escape tactic of many.

Ferocious and Forceful

From there, we would be able to responsibly come to terms with the ferocious, forceful, and vile aspects of our humanity and stop the lazy habit of expressing (and dismissing) them as parts of our "toxic-masculine damage," and instead own them for what they truly are: expressions of fear and the visceral experience of being alone and separate from each other. We give these parts of ourselves no space, no permission for expression in responsible ways, and therefore they show up as knee-jerk reactions when they damn well please, and usually in the most destructive and toxic ways possible.

What if we made that ferocious and forceful part of ourselves, our masculinity, conscious? What if it were not shamed and hidden away until it exploded? What if it were an intentional and inclusive conversation rather than only shared involuntarily as a pent-up "toxic" explosion used to defend against a perceived existential threat? What if, from there, we were able to express it in relation to the world around us and to ourselves? We continue to attempt to civilize that part of ourselves that is uncivilized rather than learn to love it and give it permission within ourselves. We do the same with anger, sadness and all the other "bad" emotions in addition to fear. It's this repression and shaming that creates the toxicity most associated with masculinity. Being conscious in our masculinity (and our choosing around how we use it,) means the end of masculinity personified as control, aggression and avoidance of looking weak or "losing."

Masculinity in this evolved form needs to be exercised and mastered purposefully through intentional practice, just like any other muscle, instead of unconsciously and habitually using masculinity as an automatic fear reaction to our external world. To reiterate, this is what makes it toxic - the reactionary use of it. In this way, conscious masculinity training is learning how to use this aspect of ourselves as people with other people rather than against ourselves and others as a protection mechanism.

Definitions of strength, power, and leadership have begun to be redefined by our culture to include aspects of compassion, connection, vulnerability and empathy. These are not traditional traits associated with masculinity, and they are certainly not connected to the concepts of "strength" or "power," as masculinity typically is. Masculinity needs to have these qualities integrated into it and taught as an aspect of ourselves that we can *choose* either to build and connect, or to break and separate, much like our emotions. That has masculinity be redefined as a dynamic asset rather than a problem to be eradicated. It is this redefinition of masculinity that will be its next evolution.

Vulnerability and Intimacy

Vulnerability and intimacy are aspects of the evolution of our society that masculinity and the ideals of masculinity need to now catch up with and evolve to meet. The feminine is often presented as the golden solution and rightful replacement for the "problem of toxic masculinity." But one is only the flip side of the other. Either can be used to build or destroy, to create or manipulate. It's a mistake to relate to one as the solution to the problem of the other. It creates a false zero-sum orientation to the masculine and feminine in each of us and in our cultural arena. In truth, the presence of one does not require the absence of the other, and the growth of one does not necessitate the depletion of the other. Both can grow and become valuable parts of the healthy whole. More accurately, both can *evolve* in the presence of (and even *because* of) the other without taking away from either. In this way, the next evolution of masculinity isn't a volume conversation, but a quality conversation. From there, the question becomes, "What is the *nature* of the masculinity that the world needs next?"

What's needed most from masculinity today has evolved significantly over the past few decades. The old version of stoic strength and closed heart that's devoid of emotion or feelings has expired. It's gotten us here – for better and for worse. In its historically toxic form, it's been a primary contributing source of violence, racism, sexism, nationalism and too many other "ism's" to list here, all stemming from the fear of losing the control, power and privilege associated with the masculine – the white masculine in particular. However, it's also been the source of innovation, exploration and feats of creation that shape the best parts of our world today, which results from the competitive, adventuring, hard-working aspects of the masculine.

In his seminal book *Man's Search For Meaning*, Viktor Frankl describes the meaning of life as sourced by three aspects of our experience: one's commitment to meaningful work, the embodiment and sharing of Love, and the practice of courage in the face of difficulty and suffering. Frankl writes, "When we are no longer able to change a situation, we are challenged to change ourselves. Everything can be taken from a man but one thing: the last of the human freedoms - to choose one's attitude in any given set of circumstances, to choose one's own way. Between stimulus and response there is a space. In that space is our power to choose our response. In our response lies our growth and our freedom. I grasped the meaning of the greatest secret that human poetry and human thought and belief have to impart: The salvation of man is through love and in love. What is to give light must endure burning. Each man is questioned by life; and he can only answer to life by answering for his own life; to life he can only respond by being responsible. Ever more people today have the means to live, but no meaning to live for."[4]

I love this excerpt from his book for the way it's applicable to this conversation about masculinity and what it needs to become in its next evolution. The "choosing" that Frankl references repeatedly is exactly the consciousness that masculinity needs today. The masculine can be the source of the fulfilment of Frankl's belief that "The salvation of man is through love and in love." It can be just as loving as the feminine, and can be ferocious in that loving in a way that the feminine does not stereotypically embody. It can also "endure the burning" that he describes and source the strength it takes to pause long enough to create the "space between stimulus and response" and give us the power to choose our responses, wherein lies "…our growth and our freedom."

When used consciously and with love and courage, the masculine is a perfect vehicle for this concept. That,

---

[4] Viktor Frankl, *Man's Search For Meaning.*

however, would require a cultural shift around what it means to be "masculine" and "strong." For too long, strength has been defined by the ability to control and have power over others. That definition has been bankrupted by the impact of the collateral damage that comes along with it, namely the absence of care, vulnerability and intimacy, and the subjugation of others. These are the ingredients that the new definition of strength needs to incorporate if we are to shift the way masculinity will be held in the future. Strength is at the center of masculinity, and the toxicity in masculinity is derived from the ways in which it is used to retain, emote, and symbolize that strength in the old and toxic paradigm it has lived in. If we are to reinvent masculinity and give it space to evolve, we need to loosen it from its terminal connection to this old definition of strength first. If strength were to be redefined as a willingness to be vulnerable, intimate, authentic and loving, masculinity would follow overnight, in the same way that a train will follow the new tracks that are laid in front of it.[5] Masculinity rides on a set of tracks called strength, and those tracks need to be re-routed to redefine strength as love.

Meeting Fear with Love

As a leadership coach, "Love" comes up in my conversations with business leaders as the answer to many more questions than you might imagine. When conversations with these (mostly Type-A and hyper-masculine) individuals turn to issues with partnerships, teams, or relationships with colleagues and clients, it invariably involves us addressing whether there's love amongst those team members and partners.

The new workplace culture is built around interpersonal relationships, communication, trust, and care. Gallup puts out a study each year called "The State Of The American

---

[5] Ronald Levant, Joel Wong, *The Psychology of Men and Masculinities.*

Workplace," that measures what they call "Employee Engagement." That's just their fancy way of saying "employee happiness and satisfaction with their relationship with their work and co-workers." They go on to statistically correlate this "Employee Engagement" metric directly with successful bottom line results, employee effectiveness, and retention. The paradigm we are talking about here is already shifting. Masculinity needs to simply catch up and get on board of this train on its newly defined set of tracks.

The masculine aspect of each of us needs to not just practice a new definition of strength and masculinity in a vacuum. It needs to also work WITH the feminine aspect of our being in an integrated way, and bring BOTH aspects of who we are to our work, relationships and to ourselves. The old binary notion of "this needs to be approached from EITHER the masculine OR the feminine" misses out on the opportunity of the power of our wholeness. We were designed with both these parts of ourselves not so that we could falsely separate them and try to be one or the other based upon our circumstances, but so that we could practice moving through the world as loving beings who embody both in an integrated way.

The way to practice this is as simple as it is difficult: meet fear with love. More specifically, meet the fear of looking weak with the strength of being vulnerable and loving. This is a big paradigm shift and the only way to practice it is to practice it. Only talking about it and thinking about it is the equivalent of learning to swim by talking and thinking about swimming while standing by the side of the pool. You might understand it in theory, but you need to get wet to actually learn it.

This practice can be exercised in almost any of the situations we find ourselves in every day; stuck in traffic, a disagreement with a colleague at work, dealing with a tired and frustrated child, navigating a difficult tax deadline, an argument with your spouse, etc… The key is to notice the fear and the need to exude strength before defaulting to the automatic reaction of doing so in a toxic manner through the old "toxic-masculinity" definition of strength (control, fear, violence), and instead to respond consciously through our new definition of masculine strength (vulnerability, intimacy and love).

One of my coaches I worked with decades ago taught me to practice this by asking myself, "what would Love do now?" in the most challenging situations I came across. Bringing this new definition of strength into our masculinity, the response to these situations becomes much more intentional and connective. It brings the individuals involved closer together, creates partnership and builds trust along the way. This is what masculinity can do when used consciously and with intention, rather that scapegoated and vilified.

This all needs to be taught and engaged early and often, with boys and girls alike. There needs to be a healthy outlet, conversation, and permission for masculinity in our culture that neither puts it on a pedestal nor blames and punishes its presence. That would require a shift in our culture that both accepts masculinity as part of all of us (male and female) and teaches acceptance of behaviors that are not defined in a binary fashion as either masculine or feminine.[6] This frees up the individual to feel their feelings without being shamed, to express themselves outside of the emotionless, self-reliant, power-hungry, controlling "toxic-masculinity" paradigm. What if those traits were taught as aspects of fear and managing fear instead of what it means to be "masculine?" We might find our way to a world where the masculine is a contribution, where it's celebrated in as healthy a manner as the feminine, and where we address the real source of "toxicity" as the broken relationship to fear

---

[6] Dr. Tali Shenfield, "A Primer on Child And Adolescent Anxiety," Advanced Psychology, April 2015.

that this is all masking.

On our way there, those of us who learned this "toxic masculinity" too well and too early need to practice in different and more productive ways. We need to create outlets that don't damage our relationships and communities and re-teach this pattern to our children. We need to shift our expectations of males in our culture to allow for new ways of expression and emoting to be accepted and rewarded.

Ultimately, however, we need to deal with the fear underlying the entire "toxic masculinity" paradigm in ways that are responsible and healing, rather than additionally reactive and destructive.

About Mark

Mark is an executive and leadership coach, a published author (*The Brink – How Great Leadership Is Invented* – Morgan James Publishing, 2014), and a leadership consultant and trainer.

As the President and Founder of Pinnacle Coaching, his career has spanned over 25 years working globally with top-tier business and organizational executives and prominent thought leaders. Additionally, he has spent over 14 of those years training high-level coaches to do what he does through Accomplishment Coaching's ICF (International Coach Federation) accredited Coach Training Program, where he is responsible for training coaches to do what he does and the development of innovative delivery methods for coach training.

In his private practice, his clients are C-level executives in the private sector, civic leaders in the public sector, professional athletes and teams, startup innovators, visionary creatives and front-line disruptors in their respective markets. His specialties include leadership training and development, mastery of dynamic communication, effective relationship and team building, crisis leadership, culture reinvention and implementation, market disruption, DEI initiative implementation, radical innovation, thought leadership and working with fear and the unknown as assets in unpredictable environments.

www.Pinnacle-Coaching.net

Alex Terranova, 39

San Diego, California

Chapter 2

The Masculinity Paradox

Alex Terranova

Masculinity is typically directed...from point A to point Z. In an attempt to break away from the straight line of goal and results that masculinity presents, I have penned this from the heart, open and free from the typical literary practices.

Enjoy.

The Past

When you think of shame what comes to your mind?

When you think of embarrassment what memories show up?

When you think about losing your power as a man or a woman what do you imagine?

There are certain things we associate with masculinity.

There are certain things we associate with femininity.

This doesn't mean they are true, but likely we have been indoctrinated into these beliefs. And when one of them is broken, taken from you, stripped from you, or you don't live into them it can feel devastating, a gut-wrenching toll that can be paid inside ourselves.

There's nothing worse than laying naked in bed next to a beautiful woman and her asking you what's wrong. She's not asking because you'd expressed feelings or shared something that's wrong, but she's asking because you aren't able to show up. You aren't being a man. You aren't performing. She might be thinking it's about her, but she's checking in. And she's checking because you aren't being the man you need to be. You aren't hard. Your dick, your perceived manhood isn't doing the one job you fucking demand that it does.

What does it feel like to be a man? Sometimes it feels like holding it all together just hoping to avoid that moment when your masculinity doesn't show up...

To me, masculinity feels like pressure. It feels like a need to be strong, to be tough, to be brave, to have muscles, to look fit, to look cool, to look confident and to have it together. Being human and having feelings isn't allowed. It's seemingly discouraged.

To be a man, feels like having to get the hot girl, the pretty girl, the girl in the flowy dress that gets the attention. It feels like having to get the girl other men want, a woman who not only looks attractive to everyone, an impossible and ridiculous feat, but a woman who can carry a conversation, has a career or passions she's involved with. A woman who's successful and focused and determined. It's not enough to be pretty or smart, she must be multi-faceted, brilliant, strong, sexy, cute, and have her shit together.

Being a man feels like the inability to be flexible… Not literally but also that, because muscles and sports and man things don't necessarily mean stretching. But the inability to be flexible in one's beliefs. Being stern, set in, grounded, feet and mind in focus. Be unwavering and staunch in your beliefs. Somehow being a man almost involves being closed-minded. Maybe it's because if you're open-minded you could be wrong or fallible and that's a weakness and a crack in the foundation of what it means to be a man. Maybe it's because if you are wrong, how can you also be strong?

Being right is part of being a man. It's ok to accept the things you know you don't know but the things you should know, how to lift weights, fight, sell, and give directions, those are things you should know as they are part of being a man.

Being a man feels like holding in the pain. Feels like pushing down sadness, never allowing it to reach the surface. Doing whatever is necessary to not feel sad. Sure things can suck. Things can be shitty, but to say that you are heartbroken, crushed, depressed, or sad, that is not allowed. That's an example of your weakness, having feelings are weak, they are vulnerable and leave you open and exposed and that's dangerous.

Being a man feels like needing to be angry and demonstrate that anger in ways that intimidates. If you're like me though and anger doesn't come easy, being a man feels hard in this area. Being a man when it comes to being angry feels like not good enough. It feels like fear and weakness. It feels like wanting to fuck and not being able to get hard. Anger and the ability to fight or to go to war or to defend a woman's honor all seem like part of manhood. If instant anger isn't part of your manhood are you not a man?

Being a man feels like fast shiny cars, toolsets, chopping down trees, and sports. Being a man feels like not caring about what you look like while also secretly caring.

Being a man feels like you have to know what's going on around you, what's safe, what's dangerous, and what to do at all times.

Being a man feels like leadership that won't quit, with specific purpose, hardcore inflexible commitment, and without guidance.

Being a man feels like you have to abandon your heart and your humanity in service of your genitals, because your genitals are the symbol of your manhood. They better be big.

They better work well. They better perform and satisfy another. Your genitals are like your personal weaponry, they might not always be exposed but people can tell what you're working with. We see this in how your manhood shows up in life like a man walking into battle with no weapon versus a man walking into battle with full body armor and heavy artillery. And sometimes you have all the tools and you know how to use them, but those so-called weaknesses in our hearts or those subtle pains in our minds leave us unable to perform - the greatest failure our masculinity can imagine.

Being a man feels like captivity. Like it has to look a certain way. You have to do it a certain way. You have to show up, perform, be successful, all in a certain way, or maybe you aren't so much of a man.

Being a man is exhausting.

Being a man is overwhelming.

Being a man sometimes feels very toxic.

Being a man is routine, discipline, commitment, and success. While we aren't cavemen or in tribes anymore the ideals of being a man and winning the war or going off to hunt and kill and carry back a buffalo for the tribe was success and evidence of your masculinity. But today being a man is measured in a different kind of success...measured in money, sex, or cultural cache.

Being a man is six-pack abs, having Armageddon arms, a barrel-chiseled chest, the discipline to do what you say day in and day out without getting bored or exhausted by the routine because the routine is in service of the success. Being a man is taking that physical achievement, which has to be displayed through looks or captivated activity and displaying it in business or financial championing.

Being a man feels like money. It looks great and hungry. It's driven by consumption and having more than another. It's driven by capitalism and taking advantage of whatever situation or person you can. If you don't get caught and you got what you want, that's extra man points... It can feel toxic because sometimes you don't lose points for hurting others if it's getting you money, success, or pussy.

Being a man isn't vulnerable. Vulnerability is weakness. Vulnerability is the spot you attack the castle precisely because it's weak there.

Being a man isn't being exposed. It's being closed off, shut down, and cut off from everything inside of yourself. It's short, powerful statements. It's faux confidence over actual knowing. It's intimidation and self flagellation over opening up.

Being a man is stressful. Being a man is pride. Being a man is being a boss.

But the thing is that none of this is true.

This is what I thought for 30+ years being a man was. Society conditioned me to think being a man was from *Rambo* to *Rocky*, from *Saved by The Bell* to *Wall Street*, from *Taken* to *Step Brothers,* from Elvis and Sinatra, Rick Ross and the Rock, from Clinton to Trump, to Jordan and Jay Z.

There's nothing wrong with these men, these names, these successes, but they are only part of the picture. They are only part of the puzzle...

So many people have told us what masculinity is or isn't. We are doing it here, writing an entire book about it. So many people have just made it all the fuck up.

So many people have put us in boxes that become boxes we want to break out of only to create another box to put ourselves in.

At the Core

The
Creative
Men
are human at their core.

Yet the title of man,
becomes as significant to one's core
as the signage to a store.

Our masculinity defined,
our feelings denied,
anger is all that's tried.

Sadness left behind
so much buried deep inside.

Harleys and tats,
muscles and money,
masculinity rages on
keeping us caged,
afraid and personally betrayed.

To break free from the bondage would require a trick.
But stepping outside the limits our fears told us will imprison
us quick.

It happens when we are young
we are blind and can't see
what makes us men
is imprinted right on our D.

Everything from movies, parents, magazines, and TV
What everyone says became our reality
Don't be a girl, be a man, shake it off or walk it off, and be

strong.

Be rough, and tough, don't be a pussy,
and when you fuck, you better beat it up!

If you want to break free,
there's only one way to be,
it's found in your heart's authenticity.
It demands your vulnerability,
to open up without fear and to show those tears.

To express anger without violence,
to paint, to sing and to dance.

To laugh and to cry,
and to fail and fall
without blinking an eye.

Being a man can be your straight jacket, bonded and tied,
a suit you can't escape.

It can come off,
if you're willing to be brave,
and find, there's so much more behind the illusion you've hid
behind.

So strip it down and take it off.
To find your free you'd have to express
what you've always denied.

What lights you up?
What sets you free?
Where do you feel safe enough to express your grief?

You must be courageous, you must be brave.

The depths of your soul yearn for this peace.

Being a man is being yourself.
Being open and kind,
loving and just,
crying and thriving,
being open to only one isn't enough.

It's the full range of human emotion that will free you and
open you up.

So stand up and breathe.
Break free from your life.
Out of the paradoxes and boxes
And be the man that takes you higher
designing that man from your heart's deepest desires.

The Future

What is masculinity from a spiritual perspective?

For me spirituality has no box.

And let's be clear, religion has a box. Lots of them.

But spirituality is free-flowing, it's pure, it's defined by the
individual and their partnership with the divine. The spiritual
box is ever expanding, ever shifting, changing, growing,
collapsing, mutating, and expanding again.

So what is masculinity from a spiritual perspective where
there is no box. No definition, no rules, no gimmicks, no
agendas?

I use the term spiritual on purpose because I am not a
religious man. I don't have an expertise in God or religion,
but I am a man who's been seeking to find truth in his heart
and recover truth from his soul about what God is in a world
that is so sure and ready to tell you everything God is and

isn't.

God in America is a unique God. Those in America who celebrate him from a spiritual or religious sense act like they know him, often like he's their best friend. They seemingly claim to know him, know the path to him, can easily tell you where you are right or wrong in finding him. Inside this path the journey to finding him on your own isn't advised or celebrated, it's more often critiqued and judged. Ironically as that might be.

And in writing this I realized something. God in America, like Masculinity in America, has taken on the framework of the Western Civilization. What does that mean? It means to conquer, to show and have power, to value men over women, to trust the written word over the orally told story, to love and live from your head not your heart. Masculinity in America, like God in America, is about being right, being in control, unknowingly living and choosing from fear, doubt, and greed. Masculinity in America and God in America is about righteousness, pretending rather than being, telling rather than sharing, forcing rather than leading, judging rather than accepting, denouncing rather than being curious, strength over gentleness, pain over passion, and ignoring one's inner knowing in service of what can be proven.

Masculinity has taken the language and the form of God in the West because God in the West has clearly, uniquely, and unmistakably yet stubbornly been decreed a man! The ideologies behind what it means to be a man have not always been so, but through western civilization those ideologies have become very clear that they support a western European version of humanity which denotes success as valued in money; the amount one accumulates equates to power, the family name, which can only be passed down through men, and the ability to further both of those at any cost.

To further those two ideals, financial wealth, typically through the conquering of land or resources, demands power, strength, and a lack of mercy, compassion, generosity, kindness, love, empathy, or any regard for the "others." And it demands that the man's seed, his tool to procreate, be held with high esteem, prized, cherished, celebrated, and put not only above the woman, but above all feminine attributes of growth, gentleness, love, creativity, passion, heart, joy, patience, acceptance, and compassion.

What it means to be a man in the West is so closely tied to domination that we as men have become dominated by our own ideology. We aren't choosing what it means to be us, to be men, to live as men, and raise men, but we have been conditioned and enslaved to an ideal that isn't serving us anymore.

We have become imprisoned by our masculinity.

It is time for men and everyone entangled by the chains of masculinity to become unwoven, to break free, to surrender to their humanity outside of their gender identification.

This isn't to confuse the conversation about gender or even gender identification, that's an article for another writer at another time.

This is about the current model of masculinity and how it's left most men including myself feeling left out or encapsulated by its rigorous thin and uncompromising ideals.

Men, it's not our fault.

We didn't choose this. We were born into it. We didn't even accept it or agree with it. It was programmed into us before we even realized what was happening.

We were taught to "Man Up" to "Walk it off" to not cry "like a little baby" or "a girl." We were quickly taught to catch a ball, to run, that we'd be like Daddy, who was already indoctrinated in these ideals. We were taught we were heroes like Superman and Batman, that dolls, the arts, and creativity were for girls. We were pushed to run, and chase, and even fight, often celebrated for doing it. We were groomed for hard work, even to suffer through it at times because our feelings weren't important. That was a woman's thing, to feel, to cry, to express their happiness or sadness.

Oh, but we were allowed and taught anger. Anger was ok. It was ok to be angry, to use our fists. We were told that we "were the man of the house" and to protect our mothers and sisters. We were taken hunting and fishing to target and kill as a means to provide. We were not taught to cook, but to barbecue, to burn something in a fire while drinking and shooting the shit. We were taught that if we weren't strong physically, we had to become strong financially.

That there are only two ways to power, the fist or the financials.

That power, strength, and accumulation are things to be cherished and acquired!

Not only are these masculine ideas but they are western civilization ideals. They are ideas also adopted by the most powerful religions on the earth.

Masculinity has become a chase, a race, and a fight. Lock up, load up, anti up, get up, and let's go.

I'm exhausted by the masculinity of the past. The masculinity of Eurocentric ideals. I'm burned out of being burned out...another masculine ideal. If something is broken it must be fixed, that's masculine also, to repair, to replace, to feel like you have to make something whole again. The feminine might imagine it to be whole already, it might want to heal it, to nourish it, to support it back to its whole self. But the masculine fixes and forces it to be whole again.

What would it look like to live in a space without the rigid lines of the masculine?

I wonder this often. And let's be clear, there is nothing wrong with my masculinity. I actually love it. I've created a wonderful space to exist with it, to partner with it, to lean on it, to push it aside and embrace my feminine. And the process continues to evolve to grow, to expand, to unfold.

But that masculine is like swinging on the monkey bars, there's only one path, it's forward or back. There's no up and down, no side to side, no off the trail or path. It's just forward, one cold hard steel rung at a time.

In direct contrast, look at what mother nature creates. No plant, no flower, no blade of grass, no tree, no snowflake, no person, no animal, no planet is the same. Everything, even things that seem similar and come from the same lineage or genes, differ. There are so many different ways, so many different routes and processes. But we've raped and plundered Mother Nature, we've taken everything from her, tied her up, put tape over her mouth, shoved her in a closet and asked her to remain silent while masculinity rapes and plunders her offspring...and all this means is the masculine is right and better.

While she might be taped up, locked up, and silenced, she isn't unheard, unseen, or unfelt. She can't be, because she's not a straight line. She's not those fucking monkey bars with one path forward or back. She's a cornucopia of all the things, there aren't even directions or plans, because she doesn't need them, she creates as she goes, she invents as she dances, she expands through experiment. There is no end, no beginning. No start and no finish.

Masculinity can't stand it. It pushes against it. We must be better, more powerful, stronger, more dominating. We must find a way to control and ravage the uncontrollable and unravageable.

But you must remember I don't hate my masculinity, I love it, I cherish my getting it done, my power in bold directness. But I also yearn for flow. I need to be out of the masculine box. I yearn for creativity, love, invention, magic, and spontaneity. My passion is driven by my feminine, but the commitment to it comes from my masculine. My love grows from my feminine, but my masculine leads the fight for that love. My creativity is driven by my feminine, but the goals are achieved in partnership with my masculine. My life is a beautiful combination of my masculine and my feminine and it's only whole in that partnership.

Every kiss, every laugh, every love, every relationship, every hug, every job, and every creation is a birth because I allow my feminine and my masculine to partner in this dance. If we don't allow them to partner we will in a sense always be dancing alone.

About Alex

Alex Terranova, PCC, ACCC, CHC, is a professional and personal certified performance coach. He works with strong, successful leaders, rebellious innovators, and powerful teams in Fortune 500 companies who are ready to boldly declare what they want, get real about what's in the way, and create the strategies and steps to generate more authenticity, clarity, freedom, and success. Through his 1-1 coaching, online courses, workshops and his book, *Fictional Authenticity*, he has helped clients earn ten times their incomes, save marriages, get published, scale their companies, buy dream homes, launch companies, build successful teams but most importantly fall in love with their lives.

After graduating from the University of Southern California, Alex led teams in the hospitality industry, training 100+ managers, opening 17 new restaurants in 7 states, and became the Director of Operations and Franchise Operations for an 8-figure restaurant group. After an emotional awakening that he'd never fulfill his purpose in hospitality, Alex got certified through the most rigorous leadership and coach training program available and read over 200 books on success, entrepreneurship, leadership, business, and performance. In 2015 he launched DreamMason Inc., and ever since he's hosted The DreamMason Podcast where he's interviewed almost 200 of the world's highest performing, brilliant, and successful leaders as well as co-hosting The Coaching Show, The Frequency Shifters Show, and Flip the Lens; A Podcast. Alex has been featured and seen on Fox, NBC, Good Morning La La Land, Yahoo Business, Elephant Journal, and many top podcasts.

www.thedreammason.com

Christopher Paige, 42

New York City, New York

Chapter 3

Just Some Guy Talking... about Masculinity

Christopher Paige

I really had no male role models in my upbringing. To be clear, my father and mother were married "till death do you part." I did not have any men to whom I looked as exemplars. I also did not trust many men or males in general due to a host of life-changing incidents that involved men external to my immediate family. Until this very moment, I have never considered this fact, but I can start to see in this moment how impactful the lack of identifiable male role models has been.

At the same time, the men in my family and life were men that respected people for the most part. There was not a designation of a way that a specific gender was supposed to behave. When I have been asked about male role models in the past, I thought that I didn't have role models as a man in the sense that there was no one that I admired more than the next, save my father. My admiration for my father required adulthood, and recognizing his adult self in my adult self.

The men in my world went to work, came home, were respectful of their family, prayed, studied the Bible, and did their best to preach God's word to others. I was never taught to respect people or not based on their gender, but to respect everyone, and life itself, because each person is a gift from God.

I grew up in a multiracial, evangelical, politically neutral environment, in a matriarchal family structure. Even though most of my family on both sides were nuclear in structure, women in my family were very dominant. Even though I was aware of my maleness, I learned from strong women about being strong, learning the stories of strong grandmothers and their daughters.

The inequity perpetuated by men in my matriarchs' lives made me want to be a better man without really knowing what it meant to be a man. I learned the lessons of distance and acquiescence from the men in my life. I learned from them how to make myself smaller to allow women to feel empowered or unthreatened. I learned to "keep my head down" and "stay in my lane," and use my talents to speak for what I was afraid to say, lest I be a man who behaved badly. I learned to be nearly obsequious, thinking that I was being supportive of the needs of my female family.

I just never wanted to be the boy or the man that made a woman feel anything but powerful and able, but I never really learned to be a man. I just grew into the body of one.

Maybe that made space for my own interpretation, but I am realizing more and more that I was waiting for someone to allow me to make that decision, instead of celebrating and participating in the ability to have my own perspective, and how even that decision plays into embracing masculinity. This had much more to do with my desire to please everyone, which I was never taught. The anomaly that I was, and still am, caused people's excitement about my future to turn into expectations that shackled me. My defense mechanism became my assumed behavior.

Being a Man in 2020

I think that being a man in 2020 is being a human with male intentions. It means seeing a world beyond genitalia and cliche. It means being able to claim your own power and use it without impeding anyone else's, regardless of one's reasoning why that might be acceptable.

A man in 2020 has to be aware that anyone who identifies as a woman is in an interesting moment of breaking ceilings, chains, perceptions and even mirrors, and respects that. This also should encourage him to revisit anything about being a man that might not really work. Today's man has to work diligently to make sure that his definition of himself relies on nothing but the work he does, the love he gives, the relationships he fosters, and what he decides.

The pandemic began to introduce some type of civility into this world that was soon replaced by hostility from angry men and women, pent up with their own misinformation, insecurities, and phobia. Claiming the title of a man means that one's political, social, and world views are not tainted by vacuous obsessions. A man has to learn how to respect himself and women, and all genders and genres of people. Maleness is not defined by how one's body is equipped, and it does not wait for others to decide how it appears or festoons itself in each person. A man of 2020 knows that his personal security is not infringed upon by others.

Defining Masculinity

Masculinity to me is understanding the skin you're in. It is strength, and virtue, and acceptance of the volition of others, because said acceptance also makes room for one's own strength. It means that the visceral feeling of being virile, of living the power within my muscle and bone, and knowing that this definition needs no validation from anyone else, just as this validation does not erase anyone else's power.

For me, when I stretch my body beyond limits, this feels like masculinity - not because of what I achieve, but that is, for me, the fullest realization of who I am in a carnal sense, which happens to be man. The physical expression of our body is what differentiates us, men and women, at least to me. There is nothing wrong in living that truth, as long as the physical difference is not the only truth that one lives. That physical expression does not indicate superiority or inferiority. There is not a real measure of masculinity because there are various methods to express it. Masculinity is a balance of strength and emotion, reason and brawn. I do believe that masculinity implies a physicality to some, but is more of a flavor of expression. Masculinity carries a husk to it, rusticity tempered by urbanity, tinged with fire, sprinkled by love for self, family and others.

Relating to Other Men

I never really considered how I relate to other men, but it is an interesting morsel to ponder. My upbringing definitely makes me question other men immediately. I start with much lower expectations of men, partly because I'm more accustomed to bad behavior and judgment by men. I'm sure that this should change as well, but life has taught me that I am rarely disappointed by other men if I am not surprised by their misogyny, misandry, or misanthropy. It's not that I have not experienced bad behavior from women, but in my experience, men can tend to be more unaware of how badly their prejudices are showing.

Our societies, in a good and bad way, seem to expect and hope that women are more emotionally intelligent, but we only celebrate this quality when found in men. Thus, I tend to be cautious, pensive, and guarded when I meet other men.

Being part of various underrepresented groups has also contributed to my reticence with other men, because my experiences with male expression of prejudice have been more drastic, to the level of life threatening.

Generally, I feel physically safe in most environments, but people can act in ways that make you feel unsafe emotionally. As time passes, I let my guard down more around other men, especially as I have observed levels of behavior that I recognize as safe. Belonging to underrepresented groups alters that way that you see life, and people, and increases your concern for physical, emotional, financial and professional safety. I have found that keeping other men at arms length until I can figure them out is how I begin.

Afterwards, I tend to open up slowly. I tend to trust cautiously and socialize lightly. I get the read from other people who may fall into similar groups. I also observe how a man interacts with a woman or how women speak about this man. There are men who flip a gender interactional light switch and are completely different people when they connect with women. All of these cues add up to me to inform how I categorize a man.

A Simple Handshake

I'd be remiss if I did not mention that being bisexual places me in a solitary plateau between straight men and men in the LGBTQIA community. I find that men of all backgrounds and all preferences tend to be confused by bisexuality and do not know whether they can embrace it, should fear it, or should envy it. Their feelings on how I love can color their interactions.

Depending on their role in my life, I may have many thoughts in a single moment about how we interact. For example, I have seen how a simple handshake turns into a moment of wondering if he thinks that I shook hands strong enough, or if he thinks that my hand lingered too long in his. To be clear, these considerations are not my paranoia - they are formed by actual incidents in my life. I've had men think that a momentary glance that might have captured their body in my head was a lustful gesture. I've had it said in jest, and with complete conviction, that an invitation to hang out was really a veiled attempt at a date or, worse yet, a desire to lower defense so as to facilitate seduction. When these types of baseless accusations surface, it so complicates business connections or personal relationships. Other times, professionally, I cannot have a "bad day," lest I be advised to "stop being so emotional," "toughen up," "grow a backbone," "man up" - yes, all things that I have been told in secular settings when I disagree or took a stand.

I was introduced once by a manager to a client as "the feminine one on the team." Even more unbelievable are the words that are said when I leave the room, or the first impressions that are related later. I have come to know that some of these statements and actions arise because of the speaker's own unspoken desires, curiosities, or past negative interactions with non-straight men. It is frustrating to be the recipient of someone's else misplaced aggression or internalized complexes, simple because of my presence.

There's also the constant interest in the specifics of my sex life from those who don't oppress me because of it. I've been asked in general conversation for intimate details of my sex life, including favorite positions, which lubrication I prefer, and other extremely personal details that straight men are never asked or divulge. If a straight man were asked these questions by any man, but especially by a non-straight man, I'm sure that the response would be consternation, not information. I blame this behavior partly on this unspoken emasculation that happens when a straight man finds out that you are anything but completely straight. I've seen this happen so often, the loss of respect or comfort that erases from another man's face when they learn that I am not straight. For some, this change in perception replaces their respect for another straight man with a new obligation from me to qualify our connection by answering any and every questions that he may have, no matter how in depth.

Gay men also can treat me as an outsider. Whether intimated or clearly stated, I face anger for "not deciding," or "not being 'strong' enough to be gay," or being "confused." I have also had some gay men express that they felt as if I cannot understand them because I "don't face the same discrimination" simply because I also date women. (I've been in my current relationship for 9 years, but when I am single, I date women and men.) Another weird interaction that happens often is that men of all kinds will refuse to accept my bisexuality and decide that I am gay. When you add all of these things together, it appears that other men are more interested in determining my sexuality than I am.

Race

As a multiracial man, there is another angle to consider. For years, I have been taught by society to make myself smaller in many situations where I am in a mixed company. I present as ethnically ambiguous, meaning I don't present as Caucasian - but it's clear that I'm a product of racial mixture. Specifically, my lineage draws from Black, Caucasian, Latinx, Asian, and Native American, so I represent the new America. Old America, though, still finds my amount of melanin and my melange of features as scary for some, angering others, distancing still more. Add to that my stature. I'm of a stocky build, to the point that I am often asked if I play/played football or work construction. Combining all of that together, I have to be aware of other people's possible initial perception of me. Again, this is not paranoia. This self-preservatory tendency is the result of years of personal experience. My olive complexion is often the darkest hue in the many of the rooms where I work, live, or reside.

This means that I have often been the "first" non-White male in many environments - so I become the receptable all over again for white male baggage in regards to everything that I represent. In offices, board rooms, and classrooms, this manifests in being watched, not trusted, "needing to be mentored," advised by men who have much less experience and success than I do. It also means that I have to temper my passion so as not to be seen as "too angry," "too forceful," "wild," or "problematic."

I still have to deal with automatically being labeled as a criminal or dangerous on sight by men of authority. When facing men with legal power and weapons, where my safety and life can hang in the balance of someone with unwarranted anger or prejudice, I can be placed in a precarious position where the only thing that has changed since slavery is moving off the plantation.

Also be aware that my ambiguity in ethnicity does not align me with any of the groups from which I descend. I am not fully any one thing, and while that has only made me feel incredibly connected to my country and world, it gives men especially enough pause so as to be noticeable. My cultural ties are disregarded. Some of those groups from which I come think either that I am not worthy enough to be included, or that I am a symbol of loss of culture. Some of my cultures see me as tainted; others see me as riding the wave of the best of all worlds, without deficits of any.

This chasm between how they view me and how I need to act toward them has created a moat around my kingdom of myself, and sometimes it's difficult to even think about lowering the drawbridge. I do, because I have gained some great friends by allowing for the vulnerability.

As someone who lives fluidly in regards to preference, I find that I have a unique dynamic with women. Some women like my company because they view me as a harmless man since I basically fall under the bisexual category. Some don't understand what it means, just as men don't. Adding to that is the complication of race in this country. This is the only country in which I'd like to live.

What Masculinity "Should" Look Like

I think masculinity should look like me. Why can't I be a portrait of masculinity? I remember that someone was describing to me a friend of theirs who happens to a male in the LGBTIA spectrum. The description included: "He is so feminine that he makes you (meaning me) look like the most typically masculine man ever." There it was, shining like sunrise on a cloudless morning, the designation that I sought to avoid - femininity. This is the last thing that a man like me is looking to add to his roster. A few minutes passed and I examined the comment. She didn't say that I was feminine - she said that I am not the typical version of masculinity.

I heard in that comment what society has taught me to fear. I didn't see myself on a continuum of masculinity. I also thought about my friend and what I know about her background, her experience with LGBTIA men, men in general, and when I circled back, I accepted that my masculinity is constantly evolving. Whatever it is, it is up to me to accept that I am male, and I exist, and the essence of my existence is the display of my masculinity.

There is this insistence in America of placing everything into a box as soon as it's processed like we are indentured servants, locked in a factory of emotions, observations, and visuals. The minute that people see something, we immediately must use our initial observation to decide the box in which this new observation fits, then ship it off via the courier of our comments and actions. I am the definition of masculinity that I know best, so it should look like me.

Money, Financial Success, and Masculinity

Money and I have been forced to tolerate each other. We are like exes that formed a company together and still have to see each other every day. We grew up together liking each other.

Money abandoned me during college, and feeling spurned, I abandoned money for a while. I lived like a pauper partly from circumstance and partly by decision. I saw how the pursuit of money had isolated some people and had placed so much pressure on others. I saw my family that was richer and how they treated us - especially my mom, who was the in-law to them. My dad's cousin told me when I was five that my mother was poor. Who says that to a child? People like that made me detest riches, but also want riches to be "better" than them.

However, I realize that all the things that I still want to accomplish need money to achieve. It's a means to an end, not an end.

I did attach my worth to the amount of money that I made, not so much that I had available. Many people in my life in the last few years have shown me that not having a lot of money, and the things that I might not be able to do because of this, devalued me in their eyes.

I was once in a relationship where I was told that money equaled love, as in, the amount of money this person gave to people was relative to how much they loved people. Recently, in the last five years, I broke a front tooth. I have benefits but front teeth are considered cosmetic, so you have to pay most of it out of pocket. The cost was prohibitive, and I've had more pressing things that required my money. I was waiting for a wage change to correct my wage, and it's been a long process.

During this time, I've heard the nastiest comments from people. All of these people have more than enough money to pay for this procedure or lend me the money. All of these people sought to make light of my situation, belittle me, tell me that I look homeless, tell me how great I would look if I just fixed that tooth.

They weren't specifically laughing about the incident, but what sponsored their humor and ire was the fact that I did not have the money to fix it. One person even told me that they were embarrassed to be seen in public with me and declined many times to go out places with me.

Their incredulity and disdain for my situation and, thus, me, was centered on the fact that my income level was much lower than theirs, and my tooth is a physical manifestation of this difference. If seen together, people would obviously know that there was a difference in tax brackets. In truth, though, could I really be hurt by ones who vapor as such? I know that I am a great person, and if someone could let my financial status determine our connection, then financial status is an unreliable measure of greatness. Thank God for that broken tooth for breaking the fourth wall of my life.

I can't tell another man what to think, but I feel that men benefit more from identifying what their success is, without money attached to the equation. There are lots of people who have money that was inherited. There are men who flourish from ill-gotten gains. Are they role models? There are men that struggle each day to feed themselves or their family. Are they not examples of what a man should do? Once a man determines his desired role or roles, he has to decide if he wants to use the road maps ahead of him or chart his own course. I think that the maps help, but the journey should be one's own.

Mental Health

We are at a point where some men do actively treat their mental health as something that is as important as their physical health. In my reality, I don't see most of the men in my world even consider it. Mental health, to men that I know, is something that you take care of when you have completely fallen apart, or when it is deemed necessary by work or forced by a partner in a relationship

Critical for Our Survival

I am passionate about redefining masculinity because life is requiring that we do so in order to survive. Women are constantly evolving the idea of womanhood and femininity. People with physical and learning challenges are consistently pushing boundaries. Men can't just sit back and think that we are great because of testosterone and appendages.

More directly, the failings of men, both those in power and those of the everyday man, are being highlighted daily, and this country is suffering because of it. Men from the old model of "money, power, then respect" give us political leaders who hurt, offend, assault and insult regularly. This gives us kids in the street without proper role models, fueled by abandonment issues, who think that being a man is about fighting, fear, and crime. This gives us middle aged men who think that catcalling, inappropriate behavior, and philandering is what makes them respected. This has taught a generation of women that "locker room talk" is acceptable, even for men who have wives and daughters of their own. It's part of why we have law enforcement officials who assert their authority inappropriately, even to the point of causing other men's deaths, because a badge has told them that they are more of a man that someone else.

Toxic masculinity is why you also have men who feel emasculated because their female partner makes more money. It's why LGBTQIA men stay in the closet, with some never making it out. It's why other law enforcement officials struggle to reel in their colleague who is out of control, because standing up can mean standing out. Redefining masculinity would allow generations of men to finally define each man for himself, by himself.

Masculine Traits in Western Culture

Courage, Independence, Leadership, and Assertiveness are all traits that the Western Culture have defined as masculine traits.

Courage is not a uniform that one puts on in the morning and takes off at night. It is the fearlessness to move, act, disagree, and change without concern for the repercussion. We have been fed the idea, though, that courage is a scene about four-fifths of the way into a movie. The leader will kick down the door, blow up the bad guy, and walk away with the princess, smoking a cigar, as the final explosion billows and the credits roll.

Courage is an everyday thing. Independence is an everyday experience. Leadership is repetitive. Assertiveness gets things done in an equitable fashion. Western culture has us believe that the leader does not care about feelings, ethics and consequences. A man's man "says it like it is," even if what he is saying is a lie. There are times that "not taking no for an answer" is necessary. However, it's like making a cake. Throwing eggs into a bowl and sorting out all the shell pieces might grab attention, but it is so much to rectify afterwards. You could just tap the eggs on the side of the bowl calmly. You still might end up with a little shell in the bowl, but it's much less to clean up.

Our Future

I see men letting men be humans. I see men supporting each other when they need it. I can envision men being able to explore who they are without that journey causing any reaction from other men. I hope to see everyone who presents themselves as male as able to carry that moniker without buckling, because the load should be lighter.

Functioning together requires a reboot. It requires men who behave badly to be brought to justice for their wrongs. It is also understanding that when a man does something wrong, and repents, he needs to be able to keep living. Functioning together must arise from inculcating respect for all, understanding that respect is required, and approval is a bonus.

Modern Masculinity

Barack Obama represents someone who "does the work." He leads, he listens, he follows, he thinks before he reacts. He uses humor to diffuse situations and make connections. He seeks to bridge gaps.

Modern Masculinity is sleek, but relaxed. It is saying "I don't know, but I am committed to finding out." It is the man who can find the nerve to be right even if it's unpopular. Modern Masculinity does not ask for permission from anyone to be approved. It presents itself in each man as a variation, like hair and skin color.

About Christopher

Christopher Paige has been dancing since childhood. He's competed in closed circuit and open ballroom and Latin dance competitions throughout the United States.

Career Highlights include:

- 16 years as an instructor and choreographer at Arthur Murray Dance Studios, various locations.
- 4 years as the Coach of the Rutgers University Salsa Team.
- TV Appearances include spots on MTV and ABC (Good Morning America).
- Zumba Instructor.

He maintains active participation in the dance community, including Ballroom for Seniors, and as a volunteer coach for youth dance teams in New York City.

He has worked for Yelp, Signpost, AppCard and other digital/internet based advertising and marketing companies, as well as a career in Fitness/Training Sales at New York Sports Club and LA Fitness.

As a writer, Christopher has been writing as a hobby since childhood, throughout college, up to the present. The last few years, and the pandemic, have sparked his foray into podcasting and blogging to bring his unique life experience and perspective to the world.

www.christopherjpaige.nyc

Kevin Wilhelm, 59

Kensington, Connecticut

Chapter 4

The Heart

Kevin Wilhelm

"It's all about the heart" said my friend and spiritual mentor Pete yet again as we were finishing up lunch. I nodded my head silently, thinking to myself, 'yeah, yeah,' as I usually did when we wrapped up another of our many lengthy chats about life, faith, marriage, fatherhood, and more.

Pete knew that I lived mostly in my head rather than from my heart. I was not very comfortable expressing my feelings or emotions. I think I feared that if I expressed feelings or emotions that would only reinforce the negative self-image I already had of myself as weak. I surely didn't want to appear even weaker to others than I thought I was!

My mind was my comfort zone. Although I had always been friendly and connected fairly easily with most people, my connections were primarily on a shallow level. I often overthought conversations or my actions. Sometimes I would even have entire conversations with people in my own head! My heart, though, always craved deep relationships. I wanted to be like Pete who seemed to effortlessly cultivate them just by being himself.

I always enjoyed my time with Pete, a youth pastor who was introduced to me in 2010, when I was approaching my fiftieth birthday. A mutual friend suggested Pete could be engaged as an ally in the work of the non-profit I lead. The more I spent time with Pete the more I wanted to spend time with him. He had joy, contentment, strong relationships, and deep faith. I wanted all of these but was starting from scratch with none of these.

Pete worked out, he built things with his hands, and he loved the outdoors. He could be competitive and aggressive. He was a man's man. He loved people deeply as his faith taught him. He frequently emphasized his faith, but I kept kind of dismissing faith as the driver of his joy, contentment, and secure relationships.

Pete was a hugger and shed tears when he became emotional. He talked openly about his struggles. He was strong *and* vulnerable.

I'll never forget the time he started talking about his love for his wife. He had to continually pause as he teared up. The mere thought of who she was and how much joy she brought to him and his family made him start to gently weep, and in public no less! I was reminded of the shortest verse in the Bible, "Jesus wept" (John 11:35).

My journey and struggle as a man literally began at birth, although I wouldn't realize it for many, many years. I was born five minutes after my twin brother, Barry, on December 9, 1961. Since I was born second it seemed as if I had already started off behind in comparison to my brother. Although my brother and I were born identical twins, he always was a little taller, more athletic, and more confident. He generally had more of the stereotypical masculine traits, and I had more of the stereotypical feminine traits. I was sensitive, empathetic, compassionate, and longing for deep connection.

We were constantly being compared against each other. Worse yet is that we were being asked to compare ourselves in front of others, often by well-intended adults such as our neighbors and teachers. I *hated* being bombarded with all the same questions seemingly all the time. "Which one of you is more athletic? Which one is stronger? Which one is smarter? Which one of you is better looking?" And on and on.

I fell hard into the comparison trap…*hard.* I was almost always on the short end of the comparison in my mind. My insecurities about my masculine identity or lack thereof persisted for decades. I only had one close male friend throughout school. We were inseparable. We were lifelines to each other during difficult times. He was a product of divorce and confused sexual identity and I was a false product of deep insecurities about who I was with respect to male identity.

So, I did what many guys do. I tried to become who I thought people wanted me to be. In my case that meant being funny, using my sarcasm to make people laugh even if they didn't realize that I was, in reality, putting them down in order to lift myself up.

Guys generally accepted my putting others down including themselves because it generated laughter and that made it all ok, I guess. My "humor" became my primary means of connecting with other men. I hid in plain sight behind my passive aggressive way of relating to men.

My insecurities deepened throughout college and in my twenties. So much so that it was rare that I was developing new friendships or spending any time with other guys. Almost all my time was spent with women. The truth is I was very intimidated by most men. They almost all seemed more confident, had their acts together, dated a lot, worked out a lot, succeeded at work, etc.

It didn't help that my twin brother was married in his early twenties and had two kids soon after. This fed my insecurities and confirmed in that fragile mind of mine that I didn't measure up as a man. Men get married and have kids soon after college (my generation and the ones before me anyway). Now the questions grew in frequency and intensity. "When are you going to get married and have kids like your brother? Who are you dating now?"

After graduating from Lake Forest College in 1983, I entered the world of work as expected. I worked for several non-profits and began to find my footing as a relatively successful employee. The places I worked employed 80-90% women. I moved a few times during my twenties, to Maryland, New Hampshire, North Carolina, and finally back to Illinois in 1991 – the same town where I had completed my undergraduate work.

Being in work environments that employed mostly women and moving around frequently became convenient excuses for me to avoid even trying to explore what I thought it meant to be a man. Worst of all this only reinforced my insecurities about my identity as a man and reinforced the qualities of empathy, compassion, and sensitivity more commonly associated with women, since that was who I was hanging out with.

You would think being around women so often would have led to a robust dating life, but in fact the comparison trap became even more pronounced. I came to believe that the gap between what other men had to offer and what I had to offer women grew and grew and grew.

What began to turn things around for me and saved me is embarrassing but true! I was 30 years old, I had recently moved to Connecticut, and my $30,000 salary doing a job I loved left little margin for anything other than the necessities. Regardless of my financial constraints, I decided to join a video dating service called Great Expectations … at a cost of $1,300. In hindsight, it seems ridiculous that I would spend that much money that I couldn't really afford on a dating service. But little did I know, that year as an active member of Great Expectations was soon to change my life.

Here is how it worked (anyone under 40 is going to think this is hilarious and perhaps kind of stupid). I completed a summary of who I was and what I was looking for in a one-page profile that went into huge binders sorted alphabetically. My photo was included. Then I had to record a seven-minute video explaining how wonderful I was. All this was to convince a woman to want to learn more about me. I also discovered that when I looked at the binders featuring my "competition" so to speak that perhaps I wasn't a bad catch after all! I admit I was totally comparing myself to the other men equally as desperate, who had paid too much money to try to attain what seemed unattainable as a result of what we normally were doing to create dating opportunities.

If I was interested in a woman after viewing her profile, picture and video I would go to the front desk and let them know. The company sent a card to the woman (or women) I had selected to let them know they had been CHOSEN! And by me of all people! The woman would then take the card back to the company, find my profile, look at the video, and then let the front desk know that, yes, indeed, Kevin was a man they wanted to date! Contact information would be released to both of us and then maybe a week or so later a date would be arranged. How was that for efficiency?

If I was rejected, then the woman didn't have to do that herself. The corporate staff would have the honor to inform me. I'm not sure this benefit was worth $1,300, but it sure was convenient not to be the bad guy so to speak!

Here's the deal though. Although it was humiliating to participate in this process, especially to go to the company and be surrounded by other men and women seeking their forever soulmate, it actually made a huge difference in my life. When the year was up I decided not to renew at yet another $1,300 a year. Why? Because I was being selected so often that I didn't need to go in and proactively engage in the process of looking through the profiles of women.

Instead, I would simply head to the company every time I received a card in the mail and learn about the women who were interested in meeting me. I had many dates that year and my confidence as a man who some women considered attractive and interesting grew dramatically.

One month later and without having to shell out another $1,300, my life changed forever when I looked across a crowded room, pointed to a beautiful redhead as far away from me as she could possibly be and told my friend I wanted to meet that woman. Seven months later we were engaged. Another seven months passed and we were married in April 1994. We were parents the next year and eventually had three kids, the last of which was born when I was 42 and my wife was 44.

I was finally starting to be a man society recognized and was comfortable with. We moved to a great neighborhood. Soon there were plenty of opportunities to connect with other men. Backyard barbeques, poker, kids sports, church, scouts, Sundays at the bar watching NFL games with my brother-in-law or other guys. I even got my wife to join me to root for my beloved Philadelphia Eagles! Fly, Eagles Fly!

I was still intimidated by men more often than not. I enjoyed family life although it was often much more difficult than I had ever imagined. But that's a whole other story...

One aspect of my life where I have been unusually blessed and relatively successful is at work. I have always loved my job and still do. I've been leading the same non-profit for 25 years and am so grateful to be part of its evolution and growth. I work with other staff and volunteers of great character, compassion, and competence.

So now I had a family and a solid work career. My identity as a man should have been more secure. But of course, my route as a man was different. My wife had a lucrative job making way more money than me and carrying the benefits. Don't misunderstand me, I made decent money and had a salary appropriate for working at a non-profit. I didn't care that my wife was the primary "breadwinner," but it did set me apart from other men who so easily fit the traditional male role model as provider of the family. My wife worked hard, was well educated, and had a career in a highly profitable industry that truly allowed us to live a lifestyle we enjoyed very much. I was grateful for that and remain so.

On the outside I seemed to be doing well. In fact, I was doing ok, but not as well as people probably assumed. My work was full of networking opportunities and my list of acquaintances grew rapidly. I was highly networked, and I became well known in the area. My family life involved lots of other opportunities to be social and connect with many neighbors and other parents.

My feelings of loneliness that I had experienced much of my life changed. I basically became lonely in a crowd. My network of people was huge and included many men, but I had very few of the kind of friendships that I craved. Guys I could really talk to, who would listen and understand, and were just fun to be around. Guys who would accept me for who I really was.

By the time I hit 50 (after a fun long weekend in Vegas!) my family had been through some traumatic times. I struggled mightily with who I was as a husband, father and man throughout my forties. I became stressed and one way that manifested itself was that I had significant trouble sleeping.

At night trying to go to sleep I would often listen to Dwight Yoakum's song, "Ain't That Lonely Yet" on my iPod over and over again. Sometimes even crying myself gently to sleep. I don't think my wife ever even knew, and I never talked about it because it seemed embarrassing. It certainly didn't feel like a "masculine" thing to do. It was odd because I wasn't really a fan of his music and the song actually conveys strength in the man whose ex was trying to woo him back. The man recognized how unhealthy the relationship had been for him and rejected her seductive attempts at reconciliation.

But I only focused on the word "lonely" in the song, and Dwight's hypnotic voice. His voice seemed sad to me and listening to it repeatedly helped me get in touch with my own sad emotions. It ended up being a cathartic and healing process that would last for about a year. It was one day around that time that Pete came to my office, and I took a turn down a new and surprising path that opened my eyes as to what masculinity and authentic manhood was really all about.

After meeting Pete that first time in 2010, I invited him to learn more about our new initiative to reduce risky behavior among young people. I wanted to recruit him as a volunteer in our efforts. Little did I know I was actually recruiting a mentor who would help me find my faith…in God and eventually in myself.

Pete and I connected often during the next two years. Hours and hours meeting in person, lots of email exchanges, regular phone calls. He sent me videos to watch, articles to read, songs to listen to, and Bible verses to reflect on. He always ended in prayer for me. Those prayers were becoming increasingly comfortable and comforting for me.

I grew to cherish our time together but his life seemed unattainable to me. I grew to be envious of who he was and what he had. He had the *most incredible passion* I'd ever encountered in another person. He had passion for his wife and four children, his friends, his parents and brothers, for his work. He had a driving passion to find his purpose in life so that he could fulfill what God had planned for him.

I began leaning into my faith with his strong and consistent encouragement. I started attending a local church that was partnering with my non-profit to feed families at Thanksgiving.

Pete knew how nervous I was about going to attend a church for the first time in over five years. To help ease my anxiety he sent me these verses before I went to church that morning on January 15, 2012:

"Let us think of ways to motivate one another to acts of love and good works. And let us not neglect our meeting together, as some people do, but encourage one another, especially now that the day of his return is drawing near" (Hebrews 10:24-25 NLT).

Pete would have had no way to know that these two verses ended up being the featured verses that Sunday because he attended a different church. Neither of us would know at the time that these verses would become the purpose of my life! I discovered that I was born to be a man who builds up and encourages other men, especially those who are lost, lonely, hurt, or broken.

Now I find myself regularly leading men's groups, speaking to men as part of our events at our men's ministry at church, and most often one on one, which I value the most. I've found my voice as a man. I am becoming confident in who I am in Christ, who is the ultimate role model for how to live your life as a man who makes a difference. I strive to make a difference in my family, my community, my church, and beyond if I can. I've learned a lot this past decade from other men about what it means to be a man today. I learned that a modern man shows love above all else.

"So now I am giving you a new commandment: Love each other. Just as I have loved you, you should love each other. " (John 13:34 NLT).

Showing love is what we are put on this earth to do. We are to show love to everyone and, thereby, reveal who God is to everyone He puts in our path.

A modern man is strong when he shows weakness;

Each time he said, "My grace is all you need. My power works best in weakness." So now I am glad to boast about my weaknesses, so that the power of Christ can work through me" (2 Corinthians 12:9 NLT).

I have come to appreciate that the traits that I had assumed were weak – being sensitive, empathetic, compassionate and longing for meaningful connections – are the very same traits God is using to make me the strong man He created to fulfill His plans for my life! I needed to struggle with my identity as a man in order to be able to understand what a real man is and how to encourage others to be the men they were born to be.

A modern man is open and vulnerable and surrounds himself with other men who share their burdens and help hold each other accountable.

"Share each other's burdens, and in this way obey the law of Christ. If you think you are too important to help someone, you are only fooling yourself. You are not that important" (Galatians 6:2-3).

If we put the needs of others first and serve them we will be serving ourselves as well. This includes serving our family by providing for their physical, emotional, financial, and spiritual needs. There is great joy in investing all that we have in others, especially our hearts, and seeing how they overcome the burdens of this world and begin to thrive!!

It's all about the heart!

About Kevin

Kevin Wilhelm is the President and CEO for the Middlesex United Way. He began his United Way career as a United Way of America intern in 1983. He has worked in United Ways in Baltimore, MD; Manchester, NH; Winston-Salem, NC and Lake County, IL.

He is active in many local community organizations including: Middlesex Chamber of Commerce Board of Directors, Old Saybrook Chamber of Commerce (Past President), Middlesex Hospital (corporator), Coalition on Housing and Homelessness Steering Committee, Middlesex Community College (Chair Regional Advisory Council, corporator, development committee and commencement speaker), Liberty Bank (corporator) Middlesex Coalition for Children (Board of Directors), MARC Community Resources President's Council, Fellowship Church Board of Directors, Middletown Works Leadership Council, Community Health Center Advisory Council.

His prior involvements include: Middletown Rotary (Board of Directors) Arrigoni BNI (VP), Middlesex County Healing Racism Coalition (Treasurer and founding member), Liberty Bank Old Saybrook Arts Festival (co-chair in 2005, 2006, 2012), Kensington United Methodist Church (church council), Collaborative Solutions (President), Middletown Blue Ribbon Commission on Youth (chair), Youth Yellow Pages (chair). He has chaired the United Way of Connecticut Chief Professional Officers (CPO) Council and served on the board and executive committee for the United Way of Connecticut. He was recognized in 1998 by the Middletown Press as one of Middlesex County's Top 20 under 40. He has published a column in the Middletown Press for over a decade. He was also recognized by the Middlesex County NAACP with its Community Service Award. In 2005 he was the Middletown Rotary Club's Rotarian of the Year.

Kevin is a graduate of Lake Forest College in Lake Forest, IL. He earned a Masters Degree in Community Education from Appalachian State University in Boone, NC. He lives with his wife, Laurie, and three children, Cameron, Hayley and Ian in Kensington.

Barry Wilhelm (Left) and Kevin Wilhelm (Right)

Kevin and Pete, 2016 Concert in New York

Kevin Wilhelm in a very manly obstacle course

Edwin Aristor, 33

New York City, New York

Chapter 5

Honoring My Masculinity

Edwin C. Aristor

Dedicated to Jean-Michel Lee Aristor,
May you forge your own unique path.

On a hot summer day in July 1991, I remember playing in my childhood backyard in Rosedale, Queens. I was about three and a half years old and I vividly remember a ton of commotion happening in the back but I'm unsure what's happening. I see blurred faces running around. I feel as if someone is in trouble, but I can barely see what's happening. I often think about this memory because it's the only memory I have of my father, Bertrand. He was having a heart attack and, shortly thereafter, he passed away.

Growing up without a father, I had father-figures in my life. My two older brothers and my uncle who lived with us at the time played a pivotal role in shaping me during my childhood. They provided structure, discipline, someone to look up to, and people I could really lean on as I navigated adolescence. Even jokingly my mother would say, "I'm your mother and father," as she had to raise three boys since she was widowed. Growing up in this matriarchal family structure highlighted a combination of feminine and masculine energy during my childhood.

As a child, I would often look up to fictional male heroes from comic books and TV shows such as Batman, Spiderman, Superman, and many others as men to look up to. They embodied strength, courage, and power. They were my idealized version of a man growing up. While I grew older, my vision of men began to evolve as I was introduced to real-life male heroes. Entering into high school, I began exploring Black historical figures who would play father figure roles in my upbringing - Malcolm X, W.E.B. DuBois, Martin Luther King, and Toussaint L'Overture - the freedom fighter of the Haitian Revolution - were a few that stood out to me.

My journey into manhood has been a combination of a bumpy road and smooth sailing but there are certain values from my trek that are embedded in my being - hard work, education, and integrity. Reflecting on those core values, I can trace back pivotal memories from my childhood that have lasted into the present age.

My mother sacrificed a lot for me to attend a private Catholic school during my middle and high school years. During my middle school years, I was academically sound, studied hard, and achieved honors, but my conduct left a lot to be desired by both my mother and teachers.

At that age, one of the main things I wanted to do was fit in. I tried so hard to be part of the cool crowd and a quiet rebel. Trying to fit in caused me to lie to my teachers, not respect other people's property, and show off to my friends. When my mother and brother attended a parent-teacher conference about my behavior, the memory that comes to mind is embarrassment and a bit of shame. I knew better. I was raised better than that.

My mother would share how much hard work she had to do to provide a private Catholic School education for my brother and me. My oldest brother would talk about the value of education and how it would open doors for my future; however, with the way I acted in school, I was squandering the opportunity in front of me. There was a moment I vividly remember when he called me out and said, "You have no integrity!" That hit me hard. He shared that I did not follow my word and that I was the type of person that would only do something that is right when someone was looking, versus doing the right thing because it's right!

Faith is such an important cornerstone of my foundation as a man. However, growing up in a Catholic household, it felt very strict at times. Going from Sunday School on the weekends to attending Catholic school from middle school all the way up to University – it's been part of my identity.

As I navigated high school and college, I began to resent the strictness of my upbringing. In my mind, if I did well in school, I should have been rewarded by going out to house parties, dance clubs, and be able to hang out whenever I felt like it. Thinking about it now, what I wanted was the freedom to explore without being held back by anyone. That also meant I wanted to do what my peers were doing – drinking, hooking up, and being my "own man." It wasn't until later that I was introduced to the concept of FOMO (Fear Of Missing Out), which is what I believed I was experiencing growing up.

Back then, I would normally have a family function, chores, or church on the weekends. When I would return to school on Mondays, I would hear about all those "epic weekends" from friends and classmates and I felt I was missing out on all the fun – the teenage and young adult drama. During that time, I started acting out and became rebellious due to my mom's over-protectiveness. I would stay out late, not pick up the phone when she or my older brothers would call and was disrespectful. I acted as if it was my way, and only my way. That was my automatic response to my family. It took a toll on the relationships in my household and my family. In my mind, it was my way to be in control because I felt I was being oppressed - a bit dramatic flair but that's the way I felt.

By performing powerful exercises with my Men's Group, participating in programs such as Momentum Education, Landmark, and diving deeper with my coaches and therapist that explored my upbringing, I started to understand that my mother was being overly protective because that was her way of showing love and she wanted to protect me as well as my brothers from the dangers of life. She worked at a hospital in Brooklyn for many years and she would walk across the ER and witness young black boys/men with gunshot wounds, stabbings, physical assaults, and even death. I think she wanted to protect me and herself from that outcome. She did the best that she could with what she had and what she knew and I'm thankful for her sacrifice. As a young adult, I could barely face that reality because I was only thinking about myself, my freedom, and feeding my ego.

I look at that time during my life with a smile while shaking my head because of my lack of self-awareness but give myself some grace and forgiveness for my past actions. As an adult and now father, I realize there's a balance of providing freedom for my son while maintaining a level of protectiveness as he continues to mature into his own man.

Being a Man in 2020

On October 19, 2020, I became a father. Going from man to father is one of the most dramatic changes I've ever experienced. It really forced me to rethink who I am, what I do, and what it means to be a man. The relationships I value with my wife, my friends, my coworkers, and my family will change forever because I'm re-evaluating what's important to me and my household. I'm beginning to realize that fatherhood is an ever-changing, gradual process that will last my entire lifetime.

As I began to make this transition in 2020, I visited my father's grave this past September on a Saturday morning, which was the first time ever doing entirely solo. I've visited his gravesite for many years with my brothers and mother but never took it upon myself to do it by myself.

I stood there looking at his grave and cried at that moment. I had tears of sorrow and joy. Sorrow because I had a conversation with him about my feelings and how I wished I knew him. Tears of joy because I was becoming a father in a month. It was a very cathartic experience because I was able to release pent up emotions I've held on for years. I spoke with him about my pending fatherhood and read a note out loud about what I'm most excited about fatherhood and what I'm most scared about as well. In my note, I shared how I wished I could hold his hand, to remember his scent, to even know the sound of his voice. I spoke about how it would've been to learn how to drive from him, to learn to fix things around the house, to talk about sex, heartbreak, and his upbringing in Haiti. When I go to my mother's house, I would look at images of him from old pictures when I was a baby holding me with my mother.

I smile with a deep sadness that I did not know him, but I'm happy to know that he made the most important decision of his life by marrying my mother. She is compassionate, strong-willed, wise and one of the most perseverant people I've ever known. I've had amazing brothers who've looked out for me, mentored me, guided me into the man I am today. It was a calming experience, and I was full of joy to speak with him on a beautiful Saturday morning in the fall. I'm committed to doing this in the future as I tackle each stage of fatherhood with my son and partner. In my most recent memory, I experienced connection, love, support, and friendship with my father.

Defining Modern Masculinity

Embarking on the birth of my first child, I've been on a path of self-compassion and self-discovery of what it means to be a man. When I think of the word 'man' in today's society, I am bombarded with images that range from those of rugged masculinity to a stoic demeanor, those with ability to fix anything or build anything with their hands, to athletes who are dominant in their respective sport, to corporate professionals with briefcases zipping through midtown Manhattan, to womanizing playboys, to bumbling fathers who can barely change a diaper or fumble with house chores.

I remember being fed these images growing up on television, movies, magazines, and even now on social media. These messages were conflicting, confusing, and sometimes, very appealing. I was drawn into the idea of being athletic, so I played basketball sparingly in the parks, participated in martial arts, and ran track and field throughout high school.

Growing up in Queens, New York, I've been on the receiving end of the "how to be a man" conversation from family, classmates, the media, and older men.

There was not always a willingness to be vulnerable and share with my immediate family - or so I thought. I was never belittled for it or told to "man up," but when I was in school, I exposed to that message a lot.

The posturing when I entered 7th grade and throughout high school and college, I could relate to it so much. I wanted to be accepted and seen as masculine. I started to recognize how I rarely shared my emotions or feelings with my male friends the older I got. We shared more about sports, video games, and girls rather than deeper topics; for instance, anxiety around the final exams, finding a date for prom, getting ready for college, trying to fit in, heartache, and even troubles at home. And yet it felt so powerful when there was someone to share those moments about my own experience which were few and far between.

During college, I started to think about the future and what would be the best profession for me to make money. I started out as a Physician Assistant major. The tough academic rigor caught me by surprise, and I was not fully present to the idea of working in the medical field. Eventually I transitioned into a Finance major so I could be a man decked out in a fitted suit earning fat commission checks, dining at fancy restaurants, partying at the best clubs, and closing deals on Wall Street. Lo and behold, it was not the best time to be in Finance when I graduated college in 2009 during the housing market crash and Great Recession. Even though the economic crash was difficult to navigate, I landed roles in Banking and Technology Services in NYC where I did close deals, explored amazing cuisine, and partied at some of the best clubs in the city.

I experienced this role of being a made man – college educated, working in the city, building relationships with people from around the world, and making a good salary – but I was not fulfilled. With a cocky and brash attitude, holding back my emotions, lacking vulnerability, and self-medicating with alcohol - I was afraid to face the reality that I was unhappy. Navigating missed promotions, self-sabotage, imposter syndrome, failed relationships, and stellar performance years, I faced a roller-coaster of experiences during my young professional career.

Leaning on mentors at work while tackling my own insecurities, I started doing the real work of personal development and self-examination through therapy, prayer, meditation, and participating in programs such as Landmark Worldwide, Next Level Training, and Momentum Education, I began to form my own definition of what it means to be a man.

When I examine influences during my college years and the first few years of my professional upbringing, a few people come to mind outside of my family. One individual who I looked up to in college was my manager, a PhD of the Criminal Justice Department at St. John's University. He was of Trinidad descent, very distinguished within the college, and he would bring his two young boys to the campus to complete their homework before they would head back home. With his trust, he would ask me to watch his boys, review their homework, and spend time with them. It was a strong example of a professional man who cared for his boys and a passion to mentor others.

Looking at the relationship with my oldest brother and my two nephews growing up was an example of being a man. From watching him care for his children, guide them, and shower them with love, my eyes were opened to what an ideal man could be. I had managers from my workplace who served as role models. The men I encountered were direct, showed tough love, cared for me, mentored me, and more importantly, pushed and challenged me out of my comfort zone to be a better professional, and ultimately a better man.

To be a man is to serve. To serve my family, to serve my community, to serve my friends. Building authentic connections with other human beings and identifying what fulfills me as a person by following my passion and purpose. What I learned from those men offset so much of the version of masculinity that boys my age were trying to embody through music, movies, tv shows, and sports media I was constantly bombarded with during my youth.

Masculinity is stepping into my power as a man who exhibits strength in vulnerability, grace in my journey, and deep connection with my emotions. As a father, I'm constantly thinking of the impact (either negatively or positively) I have on my wife and my son. I'm acutely aware of the influence I have on my family that I connect with my vulnerability as a source of strength for my family, household, and community.

The timeless quote from Mahatma Gandhi that serves as my

North star, "The best way to find yourself is to lose yourself in the service of others!"

Relationships with Women

In many cases, my family would call me the baby of the family. I was the last boy of my mother. She repeatedly shared how difficult it was for her in pregnancy to carry me and for moments she was bedridden toward the latter part of it. I have so many fond memories of spending time with my mother, either going to the flea market with her, helping her in the kitchen, traveling to Manhattan to shop and pick up items for the house, or traveling to meet her friends. Affectionately, I can be considered a momma's boy, but it wasn't until later adolescence and high school that I began to become agitated by that phrase.

Why did I shun that title?! Was it because being seen as a momma's boy was considered weak, soft, a wuss, and all the other derogatory names associated with a boy close to their mother vs. the powerful traditional masculine qualities like tough, rugged, and loner? As I navigated high school with raging hormones, I began to notice a shift in how I interacted with women. Being the nice guy was not in style. I was stuck in the friend zone when I was attracted to a girl and I wanted to ask her out on a date. The guys who had a bit of an edge with a bad boy aura were seen as the more masculine and attractive guy. I started to emulate the other guys and try and act the opposite of who I actually was during that time. Looking back - what I really lacked was confidence in myself.

I also noticed a lot about how I used to relate to women. What really struck me when they talked about how men talk about women is that much of the language used - particularly around sex - is violence-themed: nailing it, tapping that ass, hitting that, and on and on. I never thought about that before, but it is how sex was often talked about during my high school and college phase.

Even when I would approach a woman and be "rejected," I realized how much of a victim I used to be with women. How I used to "blame" women when they weren't interested in me romantically or sexually. How instead of looking in the mirror or simply realizing that it's okay for someone not to be interested in me and it says nothing about my value as a human being or a man, I blamed these women.

And I think so much of that came from the version of masculinity I grew up with in school where to be accepted by the other guys my age meant I *had* to blame the women, or it meant something was wrong with me. And I didn't want to show any vulnerable or insecure emotion to the other guys of how I felt rejected by the opposite sex.

It's humbling to reflect on this now being married for the past year to an amazing partner, and having done the self-development work through therapy, meditation, and deep intimate conversations with my wife to respect and honor my relationship with women. I am so much more secure in my masculinity and self-worth, and no longer feel the need to prove to another man or woman how manly I am through anything other than the values I hold and the choices I make.

Strength in Vulnerability

I asked myself a few questions when I was deciding if I wanted to join this group of men to write about Masculinity. How vulnerable do I want to be? How would this impact my son when he reads about his father? Am I comfortable enough in my own skin to share my strengths, my struggles, and my faults? Why am I letting myself be seen by the world in a book?

Growing up in the 90's, I repeatedly thought of the ballplayers such as Michael Jordan, Derek Jeter, Ken Griffey,

Jr., and many others who I idolized as what a man should look like. My context normally aligned with the entertainers I watched on TV, saw in the movie theaters, and listened to on my iPod. I created a fictionalized version of what the ideal man would look like/be. That has changed dramatically based on the wisdom accumulated over the years. I've learned to lead a more authentic life, I've learned emotional intelligence, and how to be vulnerable in my work, personal, and family relationships.

For the longest time, I've kept my emotions so bottled up where I was not willing to express myself because I believe it showed weakness. I've encountered demanding deadlines that I had to meet because of frustrated customers and high sales quotas that needed to be met quarterly and annually, or even combative coworkers. The amount of work stress I held in was not healthy.

My strategy to let off some steam (aka self-medicating) was hitting the local happy hours in Manhattan or finding the best rooftop club on a Thursday night, which led to more drinking and more parties and late nights. It was a vicious cycle that I used to numb myself from the pain of a toxic relationship, family stress, or a missed sales quota during that quarter. My way to process these feelings and insecurities was to use external outlets versus looking inward and speaking with my partner or colleague intimately or taking on a gratitude journal practice or even talking to a therapist or coach. I was not ready to share that side of me and it was a destructive path of breakdowns and failed relationships.

When I discovered personal development programs that focused on healing past traumas, letting go of the past, and finding strength in vulnerability – I was able to find freedom and clarity that I haven't felt in ages. My new path led me to speaking with coaches who focused on men reclaiming their masculinity. I began to seek professionals who created a space for me to be incredibly vulnerable and authentic without fear or judgment. I felt more like myself because I no longer cared about the judgement of others or the simple fact that I could be judged. It was a brave space of listening, compassion, love, and understanding. The sense of freedom was liberating, and it provided me with a level of solace that I hold onto every day.

When my wife and I made the decision to have a child, one of my insecurities that bubbled to the surface was that I didn't have a father growing up, how could I be a father?!

I shared these insecurities in my men's group, with other fathers, and with my coach, and a common theme that was reflected back to me was their belief I would be an amazing father. They would share how I exhibited the qualities of mentoring others through my programs, volunteering, serving my community, and my qualities of kindness and caring for others without expecting anything in return. They could see something in me that I had in my blind spot because I only looked at the idea of not growing up with a father as something that would deter or hold me back from fatherhood. In actuality, it drives my decisions to be healthy, to be present as much as possible, and speak with other fathers so I can be the best father for my son and the best partner to my wife.

This gives me the outlet to share my story with other men who've shared a similar upbringing as myself. To share that we as men have a universal journey of defining manhood regardless of skin color, ethnicity, religious background, sexual orientation, etc. I am sharing part of my story with my son in written form so he will have an opportunity to read my journey when he's older. He will see a glimpse of my thoughts, feelings, and philosophy of what it means to be a man. I believe this is an opportunity to open my heart and soul and step out of my comfort zone to authentically express my story.

I want to contribute to the world about the journey of growing up and how I define what it means to be a man.

Facing a Crossroads

We are at a crucible of what it means to be a man in modern times. We face a crossroads of creating a new definition of masculinity where we embrace both the masculine and feminine energies of our being. Man can be strong, assertive, independent, AND compassionate, loving, loyal, caring, and have intimate relationships with both sexes. These are the qualities I embrace and exhibit in my daily life.

The notion of saying, "I love you," to another man was foreign to me growing up. It's something you would say to your mother or reluctantly to my brother depending on our mood. However, when I started to be more comfortable in my skin; authentic to my emotions as someone who is loving, caring, and a loyal friend – I embrace telling my closest friends that I love them. To say I love my brothers is not something I'm reluctant to say, but I say it passionately to let them know how I feel and that I'm willing to express myself without judgment.

During the COVID-19 pandemic and Black Lives Matter Protests, I participated in a panel where we discussed the impact of MTC (Meditation, Therapy, and Coaching) on our lives as men. Over the past two years, I've embarked on a journey of self-compassion around my own mental health by becoming certified as a Mental Health First Aid advocate and embrace therapy as a holistic way to rebuild my self-respect, self-forgiveness and to love who I am.

Having space to be authentic with my emotions and process my feelings with a specialist has been a Godsend for my relationships at work, friends, my wife, and now my newborn son. By participating in men's groups, such as the Dudes of Disruption and the Fellas, has created such a brave space to share so vulnerably and authentically this past year. As you can imagine, sharing my story and reliving some of my brightest spots as well as some of my darkest moments of my life was draining to say the least, but it allowed me to notice my own grit and resilience and what I've been able to overcome in my life.

In my youth, I believed therapy was for sick/crazy people that needed to be fixed and not something that was shared outside the home because people would think there was something wrong with you. Not only has my partner been an advocate for therapy, my coaches have often evangelized therapy as another way to embrace my humanity and masculinity.

Being comfortable in my skin and authentic to my journey, I've shared that I've been going to therapy for the past couple of years and the responses have been extremely positive especially among men, specifically black men. By sharing this aspect of my life, other men have felt comfortable to share their own therapy journey and it's created intimacy and connection I haven't experienced in the past.

The stigma attached to therapy among black men has been pervasive which allows a lot of men to struggle with trauma, anxiety, and depression unchecked. The more we talk about it as a community and society, it will be the tiny ripple of change that will positively impact and heal our communities.

At the height of the Black Lives Matter protests and racial inequality reckoning, I shared this note with my community to take a stand to what's happening but more importantly to share from an authentic place on how I am processing everything in our community. Therapy, coaching, and meditation allowed me the strength to accept myself and share from a vulnerable place in my life.

What's happened in this country this year is absolutely heartbreaking and yet, it is not surprising. The murders of George Floyd, Breonna Taylor, and Ahmaud Arbery occurred for no other reasons than racism and hate, and these hate crimes are certainly not the first of their kind. I often think if I get stopped by the police, what would I do so I don't become another hashtag/statistic? I do my best to lead with love and compassion; however, it's heartbreaking especially for those lost lives, the impact on their families, and lastly, our nation.

I say all of this to you all today because we are a community that interacts with people from all walks of life and it's important we stay active because our young people and the future generation may see themselves in these heinous acts, and because being silent is perpetuating the problem.

I, like many of you, want to help and sometimes don't know how. The only way we can be effective as allies is if we continue to educate ourselves and speak out about issues of racial injustice. These horrific examples deter us from the amazing police officers who do act with integrity and hold the motto" to protect and serve." I certainly don't have all the answers, and I definitely don't always say the right thing, but I'm learning alongside each of you.

Walking the Walk

The unexpected passing of Chadwick Boseman hit my spirit. I've watched him bring American icons - Jackie Robinson, Thurgood Marshall, James Brown, and the comic book hero, Black Panther - to life. Representation matters. Growing up as a comic book nerd, it was a delight to see a major black actor take on a major character of my youth on the big screen. Comic books are our American mythology. Black Panther was a worldwide phenomenon and seeing such a young man of 43 years of age succumb to a disease like colon cancer brings up my own mortality.

Chadwick was and still is an inspiration of what it means to be on the court - in the arena. He was diagnosed with colon cancer four years ago and fought it silently. During that time, he gave us Marvel's *Civil War, Marshal, Black Panther, Infinity War, Endgame, 21 Bridges*, and *Da 5 Bloods*. Lord only knows what he was going through on a daily basis. His dedication to his craft is inspiring and his talent is unreal. This is an example of courage and grace. This is what dignity looks like. I can only imagine going through chemotherapy all the while filming physically and mentally demanding movies.

I openly shared how meditation, coaching, prayer, and therapy have been helping me process this year. I made sure to reach out to close friends to hold space for them. Even speaking with my mentee who I've mentored for four years through the imentor program during his high school years was heavily impacted by the BLM protest, Covid, and his senior year of high school pivoting to online classes and graduation.

In January of 2020 during a coaching session, my coach Sylvia High, the founder of Aiming High, shared a quote that vibrated my spirit and continues to help me step into my power, "The day I became Vulnerable is the day I became Powerful!"

It's getting harder and harder each day and week, but I refuse to allow the news and social media to dictate my positivity and zest for life.

I am committed to being a present father and husband, active in civic engagement, mentoring the youth, and donating to causes that matter most to me. I am inspired by all people using their voices to move this nation forward. I've made a conscious and powerful decision to return to my source, God, which I believe is Divine Love.

My internal compass is to be a practical optimist and to see the love in this world.

About Edwin

Edwin Aristor is currently an Enterprise Account Executive at Gartner. He is a father, a husband, a son, an uncle, and a mentor. He plays an active role in serving his community by volunteering and sitting on the boards of iMentor's Young Executive Board, Robert F. Kennedy Human Rights Young Leaders, and the Haitian RoundTable.

Edwin is an advocate for technology education and championing diversity, inclusion, and equity in the technology industry. Edwin is passionate about creating opportunities that inspire and empower companies and people to achieve more. He has over 10 years of business development and enterprise-level relationship-building experience. Edwin is known best professionally for being a results-driven professional with a growth mindset, and perpetual optimism. He is a trusted advisor to both clients and peers.

The self-development/coaching programs that have made a significant impact in his life include Momentum Education, RJP Coaching, Jack Canfield Breakthrough to Success, Next Level Training, Landmark Worldwide, and Tony Robbins seminars. In his spare time, you'll find him spending quality time with family and friends enjoying New York City, traveling around the world, fitness, volunteering, uplifting and mentoring others, and lastly, personal development.

www.edwinaristor.com

Peter MacLean, 36

Montague, Massachusetts

Chapter 6

Floating

Peter McLean

Maybe we can start with a story. Writing about men and masculinity just seems so big, so vacuous. I know I need something concrete, something tangible. And even though the story is fiction, it might hit you, reader, like it hits me. Not in an academic, conceptual way. But in the gut. In the heart.

Inside of each of us there is a great ocean, and one day, long ago, a great ship set sail leaving a challenging and troubling place in search of a clean start.

Seven days into the voyage, the sea rose and burped and belched and heaved the great ship. The wind, rain, and waves were too much, and the ship was split into two great pieces. Each piece sank and slid into the froth.

Many survived and clung to anything they could find to keep them afloat and give their arms and legs a rest from treading.

Fathers were shouting for their families. Mothers screaming for the daughters. Grandfathers wailing. Grandmothers praying. Sisters crying. Brothers sobbing.

Some families were intact and others were not. Orphans were adopted. Fathers and mothers who had lost their kids joined new families. Grandfathers and grandmothers sought a place in these new families that emerged.

The old songs were still sung. But less.

The old dances were attempted but the effort was too much.

The recipes changed.

The stories were not used to being told so salty and wet.

Grandfathers and grandmothers were some of the first to go. Going with them were those tales and those songs and those old and ancient ways.

The bits of floating wood that buoyed forearms, chests, and straddled legs were feeling more and more crowded though no new people were reaching for them.

The rations were getting slimmer and more meager.

The songs dried up.

The dances went completely unattempted.

The stories…distant memories.

More and more passed and sank.

And sank without song. Story. Dish. Headstone.

The pain of watching the bubbles rise up where an elder once clung and knowing the old ways, the dignified ways, the ways that always were sinking to the bottom of the great sea right alongside was just too much for most to bear.

And so.

Once again.

These floating hoards began to split and separate.

Split and separate rather than feel the pain and grief and despair and helplessness of watching their families sink and fade.

Rather than stay together and feel the pain of these inevitable losses, they chose to separate.

And float.

Float.

Float.

From a distance.

A distance from one another.

The floating continued.

And the distance grew.

The weeks turned to months.

And months to years.

And babies were born. Babies who never heard the songs. Ate the meals. Danced the steps. Or heard the tales. Babies that floated. Separately from other babies. These babies grew up. And saw each other floating. As they've always had. Mostly not thinking a thing about it. Thinking a thing about floating. Separately. From birth to death.

Just.

Floating.

Until.

A great blow came in from the north and west. Gusting and gailing and tossing the floating people about. Into each other. Into sharp elbows. Blunt knees. Hard heads. Clenched fists. All banging and bashing about. Cries. Winces. All about they were tossed. Together they were tumbled and turned.

They found themselves pushed together as the last of the unforgiving wind blew through.

The sun came back out.The gulls could be heard overhead again. The sea became as flat and as still as glass.

And now, for the first time in years, bodies were pushed up against bodies and as they pried themselves from the tangled flotsam invariably a hand would find another's shoulder and would push off for leverage.

The pushed. Acutely aware of the feel of that hand on his shoulder.

The pusher. Acutely aware of the feel of that shoulder on his hand.

Touch.

Touch.

Touch.

But touch used to separate.

Used to regain and maintain that inherited distance.

The inheritance that didn't used to be there.

And again they went.

Went back to floating.

Floating.

Floating.

Floating.

Separately.

But some.

Some.

Some.

Some had experienced something in that tangled mess of ship siding and barrel staves when pushing off of one another.

Experienced *together*. Experienced *connection*. Experienced what felt like a hazy memory.

At first, the rafts were small. Three or four people at max and without the stories, dances, songs, and dishes the conversation was flat as the sea.

But.

Over time.

Rafts of four would meet up with rafts of three and they'd introduce themselves.

They'd laugh a little.

They'd share what they could.

This kept happening.

More and more rafts.

More and more connections.

More and more laughing.

More and more sharing.

And yet. Some. Still. Chose.

To Float.

To float alone.

To separate.

The pain. Too much. The pain of loss. That inevitability that comes with rafting up. That comes with joining together. The pain that comes with opening a heart to another. The pain that comes when that heart that you've opened up to drifts and slides down into the sea.

These survivors will all one day slip under the sea's glass flat surface. But when they do. Will they break hearts? And will those remaining have their hearts rote in two? Or. Will they choose to float?

Float.

Float.

Float.

Alone.

Separate.

.

.

.

This is a story largely about the slow process of becoming culturally orphaned. Leaving one's home lands, home dances, home songs, home stories and the pain, trauma, and isolation that comes with this cultural unmooring. And the subsequent isolation required to cope with these devastating losses.

And how does this relate to masculinity? Masculinity sits inside of a culture. Masculinity gets modeled and maintained, adjusted and corrected, through a culture's stories, songs, dances, its rituals, its heroes.

As Americans, our cultural stories are being 3D printed, grown in petri dishes, and edited on Apple products.

American culture is brand spanking new and doesn't have the perspective that older, more intact, cultures have. We are pickled in a brine of Now, of Urgency, of Every Man For Himself.

And as humans, we absorb these messages and live them out in our daily proceedings.

And, especially as men, we are hardwired to serve, to defend, to honor, to protect, to throw our hearts, hands, and backs into serving.

And, in the vacuum of any meaningful cultural narrative on what to serve, what to throw all of that heart behind, we serve the story that this place was founded on: Personal Freedom.

Personal Freedom. A beautiful thing. Absolutely. But at what cost? And are there any limits? Natural or agreed upon? And what happens when we have 330 million people serving the god of Personal Freedom? Without limits? Without consideration for all the other beings on and among this earth?

When does Collective Freedom start to make sense?

It doesn't. Not to the culturally orphaned.

So, it takes a storm, a global pandemic to throw us into each other, or separate us even more fully, for us to feel that distant memory of living for something much different than our own personal freedom and fulfillment. Or, it locks us deeper into our white knuckled grip on ME, on the big ME, and the big Mine, and the big Me and Mine and At All Costs.

As men, in America, we have the responsibility, the burden, the GIFT of having these cultural power structures tilted in our favor.

So what do we do with this? When the cultural songs, dances and heroes are not ones who espouse service to the whole, respect for all beings great and small?

That's what I'm eager to find out about. Those are the rafts I am trying to paddle and kick mine over to. The humans who are energizing new stories, new songs, new dances that put something different than just Us, just Me, just Mine at the center. And for it to look beautifully unique and different and wild and boring and basic and uninspiring and impossible and naive and confusing and inefficient and slow and damn slow and sooo gawdamnnnn slowwwwww.

I trust the long and slow road back home. Back to belonging. Back to a little Pete-sized spot at the great circle.

About Peter

Here's the bio that Pete would write about himself to make his teachers and parents happy and proud:

"**Peter McLean** has been working with groups of people for the past 15 years as a coach, farmer, educator, naturalist, facilitator, student life coordinator, speaker and event coordinator. He's made connecting people to themselves and each other his mission and life work. He serves as the Area Steward for Mankind Project New England, contributes regularly to ReImagining Masculinity, and has worked with over 1000 young men in exploring what it means to be a man today."

And here's the bio that makes him happy and proud:

"**Pete McLean** is a crazy ball of beauty and brawn. All love and loyal, fierce and funny. He can't help but be curious about you and he'll learn you and all your homies' names in one meeting. Pete's as tender as he is big. 215 pounds of tender softie pretending he's not while wearing a moustache and carhartts. Don't be fooled. He's sugar sweet. His dog is Foxy and might just be the best boy. Of all the swims, it's gotta be the river. Of all trees, it's gotta be the walnut. And of all the seasons, Winter. Pete's a force. And is learning to fall ever more deeply in love with himself, and to trust the still, small voice, more and more. He can get as quiet as he can loud. As sad as he can be happy. He's a full-on human being, alive and alove, and feeling it all."

www.youngmenawake.com

Ryan D. Hall, 43

Stamford, Connecticut

Chapter 7

The Measure of a Man

Ryan D. Hall

Even though what I'm about to share with you took place three decades ago, the events of this particular morning are tattooed on the deepest recesses of my soul. I'll carry these events until the grave.

The event took place in the Eastwood Middle School band room in Tuscaloosa, Alabama in the spring of 1991. I was in 8th grade and had just turned 14 years old.

Oftentimes I feel like I'm emotionally stuck at this age. This has been the age where my therapist and I have focused most of our time and energy.

One morning that April, our band teacher was out of the classroom. Lord only knows what he was doing, but we sure weren't playing any music. While he was gone we were told to do our homework. A bunch of 13 and 14 year olds? Doing homework?

Yeah, that'll happen. I mean, I did. But then again, I had no social life in those days. I was terrified of people.

Keep reading and you'll see why.

I had a pretty unusual health scare during the previous summer.

Like many kids, I lived much of my early childhood years

with frequent ear infections and respiratory problems. When I was five years old, I had my tonsils and adenoids removed and I had tubes put in my ears.

Medical Marvel

Now here's the thing...the summer before I went into 8th grade, my adenoids managed to grow back. Doctors had no idea how or why, but they did. This is something that quite simply isn't supposed to happen.

And in a bit of bizarre irony, the same doctor who performed my surgery when I was five did so again when I was 13.

I was first alerted that this could be a problem because there were many times that I had a terribly difficult time hearing. My hearing loss wasn't constant. But on the days when things were particularly silent, I was probably hearing at around 20-30%.

Looking back on this eventful summer, I think my parents believed I was just being an obstinate teenager, but I really wasn't. For a good portion of that summer, for all intents and purposes, I was deaf.

I was ferried to so many different doctors and physical therapists, yet nobody could figure out what was wrong. I even went to a few chiropractor appointments that summer because we thought that could help me hear again.

Yeah...not so much.

My adenoids had grown so large, I couldn't hear. This also delayed my voice being able to drop to post-pubescent levels as well.

These were just a few of the many reasons why I felt like an outcast that year.

Back to Mr. H's Band Room…

I was doing some math homework (which was traumatic in and of itself) when two of the more notorious goons in the class started snickering behind me. I'd gotten used to kids making fun of me. It became my existence for a while.

The snickering escalated into outright laughing.

Then…I felt a tap on my shoulder…

As I mentioned, my family experienced some pretty significant trauma in the years from when I was 12 to 14. Some pretty nasty estrangements from family members, lots of parental fights, and my Dad's escalating drug use were things that germinated during this time.

Being the empathic soul I am, I picked up on every bit of that energy. And this was around the time I started to pack on a few extra pounds. Pounds that have remained with me ever since, more than 30 years later.

Reacting to the tap on my shoulder, I turned around and faced my tormentors.

"We've got a question," Goon #1 asked.

"Yeah, what size bra do you wear, man?" The other asked. They both laughed lecherously.

This moment left me seeing red. Smoke was coming out of my ears, and I could feel my pulse in my eyes. This is the only time I've done this, and God willing the only time I ever will do this.

I leapt out of my chair, and yelled, "What did you say to me?!" The bigger goon stood up and got in my face. This goon was already well over six feet tall in the 8th grade. And seeing my life (and a suspension from school) flash before my eyes, I thought better of it and moved to the other side of the room and sat back down.

This was the moment when I was taught to hate the body I live in.

Family Trauma

Let's flash forward a few years to 1997. I was in college when I found out that my paternal grandmother had passed away from stomach cancer.

Believe it or not, this came as a surprise. My family had been estranged from that side of the family since the time I was around 12 years old. My grandparents were incredibly conservative people. They were certainly from the "spare the rod, spoil the child" school of parenting.

I don't totally understand or remember why and how the estrangement happened, but it did. While I don't remember the details, I sure remember the drama. So much yelling!

Age and Alzheimer's disease mellowed my grandfather in his later years. But even then, I rarely saw him until he died in 2008.

I was actually dumbfounded to learn that my grandmother had been battling colon and stomach cancer for a good portion of the time we were estranged from them. That fact alone breaks my heart.

The day came for Granny's funeral and the four of us rode to Montgomery, some two hours by car. After we arrived at their house, and after an incredibly awkward reunion with Pop, I began to mingle a little bit.

As is tradition at Southern funerals, friends of the bereaved family bring over food. It's always comfort food like fried chicken, barbecue, and this bizarre fruit salad that has grapes, cherries, and peaches among other things which are coated in this mixture of what looks to be mayonnaise and mucus.

I've been to many funerals in my life, and I have never and will never understand that stuff. But it's there at every funeral I've been to.

Every single one.

As I'm making a plate, I run into this person who swore he knew me when I was a baby. I sure didn't remember him. He may have even used the incredibly annoying colloquialism "knee high to a puppy dog" that used to drive me crazy.

I don't remember the context of how this was brought up. But cousin Whatshisname says to me "Boy you don't miss many meals, do ya?"

This has been my story for as long as I can remember. Numerous barbs and jabs about my weight and my body. Some are worse than others, but my entire life I've been at the end of jokes and insults like this.

Even now in my 40's, I still get this. Some stranger walked up to me at work, pokes my belly, and asks "when is the baby due?"

I mean, it's everywhere! And I think I know why and how this shows up for me.

Cultural Manhood

I'm a native of Tuscaloosa, Alabama. Even though I lay my head in Connecticut, I still feel like I'm a southerner. I mean...because I am.

Now when it comes to virility and masculinity in the South, what do you think of? Chances are, it's one of the many Heisman Trophy winners from the Southeastern Conference. Or perhaps, who comes to mind is a 250 pound linebacker who can run a 4.5 second 40 yard dash before he separates your head from your soul?

Or...do you think of the sensitive writer with a heart of gold and a few extra pounds?

Yeah, it's college football. Something that my alma mater in Tuscaloosa does pretty well, and of which I'm a massive fan.

What's more likely to fill a massive stadium in prime time on a Saturday night in October? An epic clash between two bitter rivals, or a meeting of the chess club?

I admit that my mindset is rather middle-school-like here. Yet I believe this is a reality for many guys like me who don't fit into the football star ideal.

Again, I feel like I'm emotionally stuck at 13 years old. Because women want the linebacker, NOT the writer.

(Yeah I know...I'm working on it.)

Now don't get me wrong, there are many aspects of the South and of Alabama that I am quite proud of.

I'm a proud son of the South...y'know, most of the time.

But I never felt like I was a real "man" growing up in the South. I was never an athlete. I was never the blue collar, work-with-your-hands type guy.

I'm a writer. I wanted to be a sportscaster. While I was never the athlete, I certainly wanted to talk about athletes.

Perhaps my greatest inspiration and model of being a man is my maternal grandfather, Melborn Ivey.

Granddaddy enlisted in the Army soon after the attack on Pearl Harbor. After basic training, he was shipped out to the South Pacific and took a Japanese bullet in the left bicep for his trouble.

He survived, though he had limited use of his left arm and hand for most of his life.

After he came home and got married, he had three kids. The oldest of whom became my Mom.

Granddaddy was highly successful in agriculture and real estate. He developed a crop rotation model which led him to be awarded a National Farm of Distinction in 1987. He got to meet President Reagan during the ceremony.

I'll remember Granddaddy mostly for two important things.

First, he was the single greatest campfire storyteller I knew and the reason why I wanted to write. One of the two most notable stories that he told me once upon a time was the story of the notorious *Three Toe* - the angry bear who became angry because a hunter cut off two of his toes...y'know, hence the name. The other was the story of *Monkeytown,* where a race of alien monkeys, which looked like lightning bugs, were sent to Earth to sabotage irrigation equipment.

And on a humid and hot September evening in 1984, Granddaddy introduced me to my single greatest sports love...the mighty Men in Crimson. The love affair I have with the Crimson Tide has continued for more than 36 years and will only stop when I do.

My grandfather wasn't a large man, but he carried himself like a giant. When Mr. Melborn walked into a room, everybody knew where he was.

He wasn't loud or grand. But he lived with integrity.

Oh, he made mistakes. Granddaddy made plenty of mistakes. But I truly believe he lived his life with integrity. His taste in women after my grandmother passed away were probably his biggest mistakes.

Now, I never saw this, but this is Hall/Ivey family lore.

My Grandmother Martha died when I was in the first grade. She was only 59 years old. Ironically, she was the same age my Mom was when she died.

The memory I have of this week is sketchy. I was but six years old at the time, so I couldn't really understand.

Martha suffered a massive cerebral hemorrhage that landed her in the ICU for a few nights before she eventually transitioned to her next life.

My mom told me that the night before she died, my mom, my aunt, my uncle, and my grandfather visited her for what turned out was one final time.

The ride from the hospital was spent in silence. Nothing but road and engine noise.

When they got home, Granddaddy went into the kitchen and fixed himself a drink. And my grandfather rarely drank alcohol.

He finished his drink in silence, went into his bedroom, closed the door, and let out a blood curdling scream that completely melted the Ivey kids.

When I look at the men in my family, it's little wonder I turned out the way I turned out.

The men on my mom's side of the family are all quietly charismatic. My grandfather was the ultimate in quiet charisma. My uncle was active in local community theatre and dance. A natural performer.

The men on my dad's side of the family are all natural leaders. Look at my dad himself. Dad could have been a rock star.

Before I came to be, Dad was a touring musician in several bands. Perhaps the biggest break he got was the band he led was invited to open for a little up and coming English rock and roll band called Led Zeppelin.

Even my grandfather was a natural leader. Barney Hall was the GM of a glass factory for 30 years. And he also had his own radio show where he'd play the guitar and sing in a rich baritone.

While I see myself as the fat, shy, and scared kid who used to stay in his room all the time, I'm really not.

I'm naturally charismatic. I can walk into a room and own it without even trying. I'm a natural performer - I am at ease in front of an audience of people in a public speaking capacity. And I'm feeling more and more called to do theatre.

What's the Measure of a Man?

Well, it never has been what you are. It's never been about your 40 time or your measurables.

The measure of a man is quite simply this; your truth. It's your pure, unvarnished truth.

I could've contorted my being into that of a football player. Granted, I don't have the athletic ability, but I could have forged my body into that of 250 pounds of ill intent.

But that's not my truth.

My truth is that I AM the sensitive writer with the heart of gold. My truth is that I carry the quiet magnetism and charisma of my grandfathers. My truth is that I am a natural performer like my dad.

The measure of who I am as a man is what I see in the mirror every day. I don't have to change what I am to be my masculine best.

All I have to do is show up and be Ryan.

I'll never have a rabid stadium with 100 thousand people chanting my name and cheering for me on national TV.

But I'm just as much of a man as any Heisman winner.

About Ryan

Ryan D. Hall is an author, podcaster, and the life coach for Kings.

As a coach, he's committed to supporting men to get into their hearts and be Kings - the heart-centered leaders of the world.

As a storyteller and podcaster, he's committed to sharing stories of power, redemption, resilience, and heart.

www.royalheartscoaching.com

Joseph Bologna, 69

Oxford, Connecticut

Chapter 8

One Man's Journey Through The Tapestry Of Life

Joseph Bologna

"I find my joy of living in the fierce and ruthless battles of life, and my pleasure comes from learning something."

- August Strindberg, Miss Julie, 1888

The team of psychologist Robert Moore and author Doug Gillette describe the four archetypes of the mature masculine as King, Magician, Warrior, and Lover. Reflecting upon my own journey, I have compartmentalized these archetypes as their healthy energies and have assigned them to the sequences of my path as recognized in their primary function. A diversified field of role models would come into play as well, defining my values - some authentic, some imagined, but all very influential to a young man hungry for knowledge and direction. In the course of the next 70 years I would wear many hats.

KING

Access to the King archetype is characterized by order, stability, justice and meaning; they are capable of making decisions independently and creatively.

I was born in midsummer of 1951 - a baby boomer! I was the

oldest of eight children born to a teenage mom and an ex-military dad. He was the strong silent type - emotion and weakness from his sons were not acceptable behaviors. Vulnerability was an impossibility to consider. Crying was not allowed. I was often physically punished for the misdeeds of my siblings - apparently it fell upon me to monitor their behavior. As a result, at an early age I questioned authority and reflected upon what was right and fair.

Comic Relief

Growing up in the '50s, a staple source of entertainment was the comic book hero - Superman, Batman, Spiderman! These were ordinary people with extraordinary abilities. Looking beyond the fantasy, they were examples of empathy personified. They were pillars who took a stand on behalf of those who couldn't defend themselves. Being small and slight of physical stature, I was the target of school bullies often and in need of a champion in my corner. My thoughts were not unfounded. I realized that the cavalry wasn't coming to my defense. I was on my own and would need to rely on my own resources.

The 1960 release of the movie *The Magnificent Seven* was broadcast on *The Sunday Night Movie*, and my parents allowed me to stay up past my normal bedtime to watch it with them. By the end of the movie my new role model would emerge - Chris Adams - an imaginary character played by Yul Brynner. The premise of the film was that a group of professional gunmen were hired by a small village to protect them from a marauding bandit group; the pay was meager, the outcome bleak, but the idea that justice would prevail against the odds was the message. A good guy dressed in black! A real badass! I wanna be that guy!

Although it was a concept I admired, at ten years old I didn't quite know what to call it. In my mind I simply viewed this character as a take charge kind of person who protected the weak, was fearless, and believed in doing the right thing. At this stage I was stepping into authenticity. Since then I have watched this movie probably a hundred times. To date it is the second most presented tv movie, only after *The Wizard of Oz* – It has been selected for the U.S. National Film Registry by the Library of Congress as being "Culturally, Historically, Aesthetically significant."

Turning the Page

While my peers were on the sandlot playing stickball, I spent my time at the local library learning and yearning to reach out to the world beyond mine; to imagine what once was, what is, and what could be!

I was a voracious reader and a collector of books on every subject. My appetite for knowledge was insatiable. The Greek classics, travel, and photography books, fiction, history and science – it all appealed to me and kept me captivated. I made a silent promise to myself that one day I would visit all the places, peoples, and things I read about. This idea was continually inspired by the adventures of Homer's Ulysses and the perseverance of Heinrich Schliemann (a German businessman/archeologist whose obsession with locating the mythical city of ancient Troy nearly broke him mentally and financially, although, in the end, he succeeded in his quest).

The most impactful book I read at this time was "Shackelton's Valiant Voyage" (the true adventure of men overcoming unbelievable circumstances). The premise of this book detailed the failed Imperial Atlantic Expedition to the South Pole in 1914. Led by Sir Ernest Shakelton, a British explorer, the 27-man crew aboard the ship Endurance were stranded on pack ice for almost two years, as their ship was beset and crushed by ice floes in the Weddell Sea. Eventually Shakelton managed to get the entire crew returned to safety. One of his quotes struck a chord with me:

"Difficulties are just things to overcome, after all."

These and others were my role models to persevere toward my goals and dreams. These voices of the past and so many others were whispering to me that the world could be mine if I so desired. It is my belief that seeking positive role models as inspiration is essential to the modern man's emotional growth.

MAGICIAN

The Magician archetype is one of thoughtfulness, awareness, and insight. Anyone with skills or knowledge that may aid others could be said to be in touch with the Magician.

Be Prepared

My next role model would come from a then 50-year-old worldwide phenomenon. Lord Baden-Powell, a British general, educator and prolific writer was the founder of the Scouting movement. Unknown to me at the time, my participation in this organization would become an investment laying the groundwork for life skills - teamwork, survival techniques, leadership, community service and a plethora of subjects available to craft. Enthusiasm and exhilaration! I dove in with the spirited sense of an adventure waiting to happen. Camping, hiking, cooking outdoors, finding my way with a map and compass, identifying edible plants and animal tracks - what fun I could have!

But there was an obstacle. How was I to fund my new interest? My parents were unable to finance this project, as there were eight of us and it wasn't a priority. Uniforms, camping equipment, etc. was not in the family budget. I would have to figure out a way to make this possible. It was time for self-motivation and tenacity. Desire and need were the motivating factors - I would do whatever it took to succeed: mow lawns, a paper route, babysit, odd jobs. For one summer (when I was twelve) I even convinced the manager of the local Cumberland Farms to hire me to load the milk delivery every morning for $3.50 a week. All these efforts eventually allowed me to meet my goals.

I was involved in the program long enough to attain the rank of First Class. That milestone and its rigorous requirements, although satisfying, was not the end game I had in mind. My goal had been to achieve the rank of Eagle Scout but unfortunately the neighborhood troop charter was not renewed. Falling short of my goal, although through no fault of my own, proved a palpable disappointment. That being said, my sense of competence in my own abilities left me secure in the knowledge that my newly acquired skills and talents were valuable to myself and others. I had gotten a taste of leadership and independence. A large part of the program was to impart skills I had learned to others.

Looking in the rearview mirror I imagine if all boys had learned the basic skills and ideals of the Scouting program, they would later in life be more prepared to handle a great deal of life's challenges, disappointments and triumphs with a better sense of self-worth.

My experience wasn't simply learning to tie knots or use a compass – rather the bigger picture was to problem solve, to untie the knots, navigate in a changing and complicated world, and to live the Scout Motto - "Be Prepared!"

WARRIOR

The Warrior archetype is a doer, not a thinker. The mission is the goal; putting emphasis on this as opposed to his relationships. He is detached from life, and has an infinite ability to withstand psychological and physical pain in pursuit of his goal. Far from being a pushover or bully, the Warrior sets boundaries and makes his needs known constructively.

It's Only Rock 'N' Roll

Rounding the corner to my early teen years…waiting in the wings would be my next role model, the legendary rock god Jack Bruce - singer, songwriter, musician, and showman of the group Cream.

The British Invasion was permeating the landscape, spear headed by The Beatles. I was fascinated with the music, the culture, the energy! Like everyone else my age I spent my time buying records, watching performances, and imagining myself on a stage in a band. I remember thinking, "that looks fun - I can do that!"

My uncle lent me money to buy a guitar and once again I felt that same rush of enthusiasm and exhilaration. Unable to afford lessons, I became self-taught, learning my instrument every available moment, my fingers constantly bleeding and sore.

Friends were going to movies, car hops, and dances. My teen desires were redirected toward a passion for making music. I practiced relentlessly. I was fortunate enough to connect with like-minded musicians from the neighborhood. It was a small town - everyone seemed to know everyone. Our focus and perseverance was eventually rewarded with an opportunity to showcase our talents. We proceeded to record, tour, and live the rock 'n' roll life (defined as sex, drugs, perform, rinse, repeat)! Working and living with an assortment of talented, sometimes ego-driven personalities was a daunting exercise in patience, compromise, and intestinal fortitude. To quote Charles Dickens - "It was the best of times, it was the worst of times, it was the age of wisdom, it was the age of foolishness."

My original sense of freedom eventually gave way to encapsulation. The dark underside of the business was starting to cause destruction and bullied its way into the part of me that denied me the "want" to continue this line of work.

Talent was becoming overshadowed by greed, power, and unfair business practices - things I would normally not tolerate. The chaos was further fueled by the beginnings of a drug and alcohol addiction. My sense of worth and value seemed to be in flux; the runner was stumbling, and I felt it was time to move on!

LOVER

The Lover archetype is described as having a general appreciation of life - from great food and warm friendships to the magnificence of nature - in ways that others cannot. He is in touch with his surroundings in a way that lends meaning to the lives of himself and others.

Sandcastles and Steel Walls

There were short-lived relationships, marriages, and divorces. Looking back on these unions I can see that I was sometimes in the rescue business rather than the "in love" business. The one constant threat plaguing me throughout this period was my battle with the aforementioned addictions which greatly affected my decisions and behaviors. I was not clear-minded or able to juggle with others and their demons. I was unrecognizable to myself!

Eventually, with the support of a reputable program I was able to get a handle on the agents of my distress, but a trail of heartbreak was left in the wake. There were times when I felt like a hamster on a wheel. Life was passing me by, and I felt as if I was waiting to start something, anything, again and again.

One of the marriages produced two daughters, another produced two sons. Over time both daughters and I became estranged due to a series of circumstances beyond my control. Another set of circumstances allowed me custody of the boys.

Having the boys back in my orbit full time was a life-changer for me, as well as for them. Despite personal setbacks and direction changes, my ability to recognize opportunity and to seize it was a strength I thought I had lost. I felt once again emerging in me the inner desire to be the best me, not settling for less.

It was now my turn to become a role model. I attempted to fill their world with the things that had once influenced mine – books, music, and adventures. Their personalities gravitated to the things they each felt most comfortable with – I simply made the tools available. They succeeded in their own way and time. Both became voracious readers with a flair for writing capabilities. Both joined and completed the Scouting program. I'm the proud father of two Eagle Scouts. The Eagle Scout Achievement required completion of 21 Merit Badges – both achieved 54. They continue to live by its learned principles and to care for others in an unselfish way.

They engaged in a healthy dose of sibling rivalry. I, knowing the pangs of only having myself to rely on at that age, constantly reminded them to appreciate and support one another. I made a conscious effort to rule their disputes with a strict but fair policy – they were encouraged to think through, do the right thing, and then stand by their decisions.

I made every attempt to remove the negatives I grew up with and to applaud their achievements. They now both have children and have become wonderful role models in their own right. They are my finest achievements!

Changing Lanes

All quiet on the home front – the boys having moved out and on with their new families left me with the opportunity to fulfill my own boyhood dreams. For the next 20 years I would travel the globe experiencing all the places and things that enchanted me as a young boy. My bucket list was quite extensive. I photographed my adventures and I came to realize the mantra was true, "Better to see something once than to hear about it a thousand times."

And what a journey it became! My travels kept me in a state of awe and wonder! With each new destination I left a piece of me in these faraway lands and each time brought a piece of the new experience home with me. Travel changes one – where the local playground was once my world, the entire world was now my playground!

Along the adventure routes my experiences included riding a camel through the Sahara Desert, walking a portion of the Great Wall in China, climbing Mayan structures in Mexico, on a safari and visiting the Masai Mara tribe in Kenya, Africa, driving a go-kart through the streets of Tokyo, Japan, sailing on the Nile River in Egypt, visiting holy sites in Cambodia, Thailand, Vietnam, India, Turkey,Italy and many other locations across Europe. Oh, and of course a visit to Bologna in Italy, while stopping along the way throughout the country's museums, and art galleries. I am frequently asked which destination was my favorite? I answer...the next one!

In 2020, the COVID-19 pandemic put a temporary hold on my continuing travel plans. I was recently (finally) retired and was not quite sure what would fill the void or come next. Through a chance encounter I was reunited with a childhood friend. She was now an accomplished writer, a professor at the local university and very active in her church, and community. Her latest ambition was to write a book on spirituality. I offered her the use of my travel photographs for her project. Our collaboration began, and working on this project with her was bringing me to another level of transformation once again. With each transformation over time I had been making a new set of agreements I wanted myself to live up to. She calls it my Code of Conduct, a trait I had always adhered to but hadn't labeled. Simply put, it was the principle of bringing my best "me" to the game. I have learned to love who I have become and my connections to those I love have become stronger.

My participation in the writing of this piece is due to all of her continuing influence to tell a story of the importance of how in society today we see many children raised without a relationship with their fathers. My wish is to share with men the significant value and emotional joy this has brought to my life. Being a role model to my sons is the gift that keeps on giving as I watch them share some of these values and principles with my grandchildren.

Passing the Baton

All men have the capacity to leave a positive legacy. In summary, the role models that influenced my life helped me to grow in a direction that in effect have benefitted my sons as well as the people that have crossed my path on my journey. When we invest in our own experiences and develop meaning in our life we invest in the future. The biggest lesson I have learned is that it takes great courage to be vulnerable.

"The mystery of life is that we don't know how our story ends, but we can plant seeds today for the future we desire, and we can find comfort in our hopes for tomorrow." - Randi G. Fine

Receiving the invitation to join this project has allowed me to dig deep inside myself to examine my past, opening doors I thought were locked a very long time ago, never to be open again. This self examination has been both painful and liberating. I wish to thank Davidson Hang for creating this project and Green Heart Living for allowing me this platform.

About Joseph

Joseph Bologna purchased his first camera at the age of 13. His thoughts were to photograph life extensively in order to 'freeze time.'He combined photography with his other interests which included reading, traveling, and music. Embarking on a career as a rock artist he photographed events as he toured with many acts.

In the 80's his photography centered on his growing family, capturing his children's events. At this time he also engaged in photographing community events, weddings, and portraiture.

In 2005 he began traveling the world photographing the people, places, and things he had read about in his youth. To date, he has visited 26 countries and taken over 90,000 photos. His work has been seen in travel magazines, private companies, and businesses.

He is a Top 10 Popular Photographer in Viewbug and has been peer-awarded over 9,000 times. Recently his works have been awarded the 2020 People's Choice, the 2020 Top Shot, and the Elite Award. He is currently collaborating on a three-book series featuring selected photos and original writings as well as featuring a chapter in a collaborative authors' work on masculinity in 2021.

Joseph at 15

Promo Photo 1973

Joseph On Tour 1975

Photographing Egypt 2018

Davidson & Samantha

New Brunswick, New Jersey

Chapter 9

Forgiveness is a Gift

Davidson Nguyen Hang

Masculinity is an interesting topic for me. I never saw myself as a masculine guy growing up, but as I've delved deeper into my true, authentic self, I've realized that I have become a man who impacts thousands of lives daily.

Being vulnerable is one of my superpowers, and I'm grateful for all of the opportunities that have come my way to be able to help lift others up.

I want to share with you defining moments that have significantly impacted me and whom I choose to be for the world.

I'm a huge podcast nerd, so when I listen to Tim Ferriss, Rich Roll, Lewis Howes, Tony Robbins, and other men who openly share their depression and disempowering beliefs, it warms my heart to know that I'm not alone. Going through the Hero's Journey is a part of being a man. I was grateful for the trauma when moving away to a completely different state where I didn't know anybody. Those times of depression, where I felt so lost and unsatisfied with my decisions and choices, led me to be a pretty fantastic career coach.

I remember sitting through Accomplishment Coaching weekends (a year long extensive professional development/

coaching program) crying my heart out, processing how much I missed my family and friends, and how all of these moments played a crucial part in becoming Davidson.

Three moments that drastically affected my life but were a blessing in disguise was when I was laid off three separate times working at jobs I was not passionate about. These helped me revise my career goals and helped me want to take responsibility and ultimately be a better person. It was so bad that during one of the Wednesday morning standing meetings, the VP of Sales gave me a clock as a present because I was late so often. All of the times when people have projected and said I would never make it to Dental School or that I need to get my shit together fueled this passion and desire to succeed in life. People always ask me what drives me to want to do so much and I say "it's because I've failed at so many things in life that I told myself that I never want to encounter the heartbreak I had when I was laid off for lack of performance."

I would say I'm certainly a late bloomer. I never did well in school, and I felt like I didn't have many close friends consistently. I always felt like an outsider. I was told that I was Asian enough for Asians, and of course, not fitting in because of my eyes and skin color made me unable to feel truly comfortable around White people.

I realized my need to meet new people and win them over is also my kryptonite. That's why more recently, I've spent a lot of time creating these communities where I get to have these vulnerable conversations where men can talk about how hard it is being a father or if they are afraid of marriage.

I was so afraid of marriage - being tied down to someone. I recently got married this year, and I remember saying to myself one day - why would anyone subject children to this cruel, cruel world? Although I'm quite optimistic nowadays, I remember always blaming the world for all of my problems. Why was I short? Why did I grow up living off of government assistance and food stamps?

I have learned to shift the question around, and it starts with, well what could I be grateful for today? Who do I have around me that lifts me up? How can I be more like them? Zack Mulhall, one of the guys I look up to, always has a beaming personality. Even though he's laser-focused, he is present when he is with you. Edwin Aristor - another one of my closest friends, who has a billion-dollar smile/laugh, is always doing what he can to help everyone else around him be the best possible version of themselves. Now I'm continually asking myself, "How can I lift others up?" Instead of always thinking about Davidson, whenever I am in service of another human being, I feel much more connected to the world.

Like many men - I always thought about athletes and being in shape as a man. I'm going to be honest and put it out there that I can be quite judgmental with people who are overweight. It brings me back to when I was in fifth grade, and I came in last in the mile in school. I remember feeling so defeated, and from that day on, I joined Cross Country, Spring Track, and Winter Track. One of my favorite memories in life is completing the Spartan Beast. I do endurance races, and it started because of my asthma. I started noticing a trend that I tend to dive into whatever I perceive I am weak at.

Being voted most reserved in the fifth grade in the yearbook has changed me because I didn't want to be someone who people couldn't relate to. It took me a couple of years, but I finally became very social. This pandemic has helped me see that it's hard for me to be by myself. For the last seven months or so, I have been by myself more, often hiking by myself. Before that, I never did anything by myself, and if I did, I would be depressed. It's funny how you can feel lonely in a city of eleven million people like Manhattan. I remember eating my problems away. When I first started seeing a therapist - I never thought that I would have a life making the type of money I am and even writing this book. I was never a great writer, or at least that was my story. I realized that having this disempowering belief was not serving me, so I started writing more and putting myself out there. Not everything you put out in the world will vibe with it, and that's just life.

I used to take feedback so personally, and I still do, but at least now I know it's coming from a good place. You can choose what you want to do with that feedback. Not all feedback is created equal, as well. Everything someone says is a projection. I know every time I judge someone for being overweight, it's because I personally am not comfortable in my own skin. I look back to those days where I felt so helpless or weak from being last, even in things like flexibility - it took me a while to realize that flexibility is sexy. I find myself going to yoga classes, and most of the time being one of the few men who attend these classes.

My relationship with money has been one of the most challenging and, at the same time, uplifting relationships. In our society, money still means a lot, and sometimes people equate money with happiness. Growing up as a child of parents who were refugees, I can see why money is talked about so much. I remember when my grandmother came to observation day during one of my coaching programs, and the first thing she asked was, "Can you make good money as a coach?" I assured her that you could. Growing up in a third world country was not easy for my family. My mother grew up without a father most of her life. He died during the war. He was an English Interpreter for the US soldiers during the war. Although I'm sad that I was never able to meet him, I'm glad that my grandmother, uncle, and mother tried their hardest to escape Vietnam to live in a country with more freedom, choices, and opportunities.

On my father's side, my grandfather was not very faithful and for my grandmother to raise twelve kids by herself was not easy. I'm very fortunate that they escaped the Vietnam War. Clearly, it was a traumatic time since no one talks about it. Having compassion for my father's decision, I can see that he followed in my grandfather's footsteps of wanting to be free and explore without being tied down.

I have noticed that every time I traveled to another country or did something on my own. It would be nice for a little bit, but I would get lonely again. I would miss Samantha - my wife. I'm not ashamed to be myself around her, and we have corny pet names, and that's okay.

Tony Robbins says masculine energy is getting stuff done. I'm grateful that I have a bias towards action, as many would say. Being a doer, I have realized that it's equally as important to focus on the being. Who do I want to be in the world? Reflecting in a journal writing down and digging into my thoughts, and what I'm proud of, excited about, and grateful for every day helps me live a happier, more fulfilled, intentional life.

I'm lucky that even though I leverage my masculine energy to get things done, I can also be compassionate and leverage my emotions to bring out passions in all of my projects and activities.

Mental health within men is something I am passionate about because I relate to feeling so lost, and I'm so grateful that my first coach Chris Wong posted on Facebook asking if anyone was interested in a sample coaching session.

I never thought I would be writing a book about this topic five years later. I'm so grateful that in five years I've accomplished more than the twenty-eight years before that, thanks to continuous reading and being curious about my judgments of myself and the world.

How you treat others is a reflection of how you treat yourself. Many of us are not so kind to ourselves. Writing down what I enjoy about my life and what makes me happy day to day is a practice that has served me well in being content with everything that is happening for me.

These are practices I would love to challenge you to take on:

Daily gratitude exercises in your journal with an extra bonus if you can share it publicly.

Meditation - I never thought of myself as a meditator. It just seemed so out of reach, and at times, it's still a challenge for me to make it a regular practice, but on the days I do meditate, I'm a bit kinder to myself and everyone else around me.

Mike Hard, a former CEO when I was working at BountyJobs, used to say, "Assume positive intent." How many of us jump to the conclusion that people have malicious intent, especially at work with people who you don't see eye to eye with? Are there any assumptions I have about people based on the past?

This pandemic could be one of the best things that has happened for society. Many of us in Western Culture were taught to keep getting promoted and work hard to pay for your kids' education to go to college. How many of our parents were so busy putting food on the table that they could not attend their kids' recitals and practices?

LinkedIn is leading the way by announcing that we will be

fifty percent work from home for all employees. That's beautiful! To be able to drive my kids to their practices and be there for them while still maintaining an excellent career is the dream. I'm excited that people and companies are starting to take a look at how we can be both great parents and still excel in our careers. We all know that when there is balance, employees are happier, and people perform optimally.

I wanted to share my takeaways from creating my men's group and the lessons from our conversations so far. To provide context, I started a men's group with twelve of my closest friends that I thought would be interested in having more profound relationships with other men. I listened to a podcast interviewing Colin O'Brady, one of the guys I look up to. He was a part of a group called the Fellas where once a month, one of the members has a spotlight. We also have a buddy system to get paired up with someone new every month and share goals to hold each other accountable. I also have a spreadsheet listing all of my goals for the Fellas to hold me accountable to what I say I want to create in the world.

For ninety minutes, one of the guys pours his heart out and discusses everything that is affecting him personally, professionally, and mentally. Whether it's dealing with a breakup or answering the question of why am I so hard on myself? The Fellas provide a space where you can be truly authentic and open. The other members ask questions and provide feedback to help the Fella be curious about some of their automatic ways of being and how to disrupt that. It's truly a touching and powerful feeling when you can sit aside, not say a word, and be able to see the magic unfold.

When men connect and are not afraid to say things like, "I love you," and "I got your back," we do not need to turn to violence or take it out on others. I genuinely believe that when given a space, we have awareness around things that make us angry. We no longer make anger a bad thing, and it no longer controls us. There have been so many moments where I would be so mad in college that I would punch holes in walls. If I had the space to share my feelings, I would not have resorted to these moments of anger and frustration. Communicating with yourself and others is critical, and it's a skill that can be uncomfortable at first.

Sharing myself openly with my wife has taken so long because I was afraid. I told myself if my dad would not stick around for me, who can I trust? I would chat with many women to become more of a man, but I was too afraid to talk and share vulnerability with my partner. I'm grateful that we are opening up and that I can share my deepest insecurities with her. Of course, there is a possibility that I can get my heart broken, but there is so much possible when I live a life of courage, love, and affection. I try to show words of gratitude and love every time I encounter someone who has impacted my life. I know for me, it always feels good to be acknowledged. Being able to acknowledge people is one of the powerful tools in the world because when you truly feel heard, you feel like you can move on and not dwell on the past anymore.

I dream of a world where every man can have a men's group where we talk about real things, not just football and superficial things. The feeling I get from our monthly calls when we can joke and be ourselves is like no other. We do not need to over-inflate our accomplishments. We can truly just be. My relationships with Brandon Ngai, Jeff Zacharski, and Edwin Aristor are examples. I can tell them that I love them, and I genuinely mean it. There are no awkward feelings or thinking about, as a man in society, I don't think you're supposed to say that. I hug them and don't feel weird that I'm showing physical displays of affection.

Being independent is something I used to be proud of because that's what society tells us we should do in Western Culture. Don't get me wrong, I do love traveling to a different state attending conferences in Austin, TX or Columbus, OH, but once I let go of the belief that I am independent, I could truly be able to ask for help when I needed it. Thank God, my parents and my in-laws are kind enough to support me when I need it. Things come up, and life doesn't go the way you plan, but that's why it's beautiful to be supported. You grow by giving, and there is an innate sense of connectedness the more you give in the world. It almost doesn't make sense logically.

Whenever I am feeling down, and I feel like I'm not being responsible financially or whatever self-disempowering belief I have about myself, I turn to giving by volunteering and helping someone else. That automatically lifts my mood, and I feel whole again. I would recommend volunteering to anyone who has never volunteered or hasn't in a while. I promise you that you will feel a hundred times better.

I used to think that men had to be athletic, or that the better provider they are for their families, the better man they are. Although financial security is one of the traits of being a man, I have learned that being authentic and not being afraid to say I love you to your wife in front of the kids is equally as important. Being able to show emotions does not mean weakness, as society shows us in movies and TV.

The Modern Masculinity is to be someone who can express his feelings no matter who is watching. He is not afraid to show physical displays of affections to others and his male friends. I envision a future where therapy is equally as prominent as going to the gym. Going to the gym for my mind has been one of the best decisions I've ever made. Because of the stigma with therapy - I used to be afraid to tell people that I go to therapy. I still go to therapy even though it's five years later, to be able to have a space where I can express how I'm feeling. I'm able to go about life and crush, knowing that I have the support and that I'm not going crazy.

Validating your experiences in a public setting can be freeing. I used to think that no one could possibly understand what I'm going through, because, "my situation is different." Suffering, pain, love, anger, and jealousy are all normal emotions. The more we suppress our feelings, the more they come out eventually, sometimes in explosions or by taking it out on someone else. I forgive my father and mother for all of the arguments they had with each other. Although there were some very uncomfortable situations we witnessed as children growing up, I know that if it weren't for those moments, I wouldn't be writing this passage right now, sharing openly with you all.

My call to action request is for all of you to deeply explore the things that trigger you and why you think that is. Are you willing to forgive and move on from the past?

These are the questions I often think about that have served me well in life.

1. Who do I want to be today? (Usually, in the morning, set aside 15 minutes to journal openly about your feelings and things that are going on).

2. How can I get myself into a higher energy state? (meditation, hiking, doing a bunch of push-ups.)

3. Who do I want to acknowledge today? Can I send someone a handwritten card or a text message saying that I'm thinking of them?

4. Who are some of my role mentors, and what small actions can I take to model their behavior?

5. Hug yourself. How many times have you been hard on yourself? It looks weird to do this, but it's a simple practice that works.

6. Make a good shit list of all of your accomplishments for the day before you go to sleep. (Shout out to William Lee for suggesting this one for me.) You'll start to realize that you accomplished a lot more than you think.

About Davidson

Davidson Hang is currently an Account Executive at LinkedIn Learning Solutions. He is a mentor, a husband, son, nephew, cousin and is also a career/life coach. In his free time, he volunteers for Orphans Future Alliance, BuildOn, Pencil, IMentor, Streetwise Partners, and loves to give back to the community. He has been in technology sales for over nine years now and loves to help people heal their trauma.

The self development/coaching programs that have made the biggest difference for him are Accomplishment Coaching, Next Level Training, Landmark Worldwide, and Tony Robbins seminars.

Davidson is also a YouTuber, author, Blogger, Podcaster, and public speaking motivational coach.

In his spare time, he is a wellness champion at LinkedIn, Toastmasters officer at Microsoft and LinkedIn, involved in Pi Delta Psi, and regularly writes articles about self development, coaching and sales.

www.DavidsonHang.com

Davidson with his Sister Jenny

Davidson and Samantha's Wedding Day
with Good Friends Pritika and Sumit

About Green Heart Living

Green Heart Living's mission is to make the world a more loving and peaceful place, one person at a time. Green Heart Living Press publishes inspirational books and stories of transformation, making the world a more loving and peaceful place, one book at a time.

Whether you have an idea for an inspirational book and want support through the writing process - or your book is already written and you are looking for a publishing path - Green Heart Living can help you get your book out into the world.

You can meet Green Heart authors on the Green Heart Living YouTube channel and the Green Heart Living Podcast.

www.greenheartliving.com

Green Heart Living Press Publications

Grow Smarter: Collaboration Secrets to Transform
Your Income and Impact

Your Daily Dose of PositiviDee

Transformation 2020

Transformation 2020 Companion Journal

The Great Pause: Blessings & Wisdom
from COVID-19

The Great Pause Journal

Love Notes: Daily Wisdom for the Soul

Green Your Heart, Green Your World:
Avoid Burnout,
Save the World and Love Your Life

Made in the USA
Middletown, DE
15 April 2021

37606917R00096